Paul Beashel

Andy Sibson

John Taylor

SPORT examined

Teacher
Support
Pack

for
Edexcel

Published in 2004 by:
Nelson Thornes Ltd
Delta Place
27 Bath Road
CHELTENHAM
GL53 7TH
United Kingdom

04 05 06 07 08 / 10 9 8 7 6 5 4 3 2 1

A catalogue record for this book is available from the British Library

ISBN 0 7487 7727 X

Illustrations by Roger Fereday, David Eaton and Pantek Arts Ltd

Page make-up by Pantek Arts Ltd, Maidstone, Kent
Printed in Great Britain by Antony Rowe

Contents

Welcome to the *Edexcel Sport Examined Teacher Support Pack*. We are very excited about this book. We have embraced the latest ideas about teaching and learning styles and developed a wealth of practical activities to encourage active learning. We hope that you will be equally enthusiastic about taking this more interactive approach to the subject.

Many of the activities have been trialled with GCSE groups and have both stimulated thinking and encouraged the full participation of all students. Recognising that we all learn in different ways, we have designed the activities to utilise a range of learning styles. The inclusion of starter exercises, including Ten-Minute Teasers, will assist you in the planning of three-part lessons.

What is in this book?

The *Edexcel Sport Examined Teacher Support Pack* provides a complete reference for GCSE PE teachers and students. It includes:

- **Ideas for enhancing learning** These include starter exercises and activities to encourage the development of thinking skills to assist the learning of topics.
- **Activity worksheets** These are designed to support a variety of learning activities for students of all abilities. They are not intended as mere form-filling exercises. The full value of the activities is only realised if time is given to students to allow them to think, discuss and apply the concepts involved. The sheets are referenced in the textbook.
- **Revision guide sheets** These contain diagrams and topic information that enable students to produce their own personal revision guide containing all of the information needed for success at GCSE. All sheets contain page references to the textbook.
- **Mark schemes** Exam-style questions appear at the end of each section of the textbook. They may be used to evaluate learning at the end of a topic and provide valuable examination technique practice.

How to use this book

Schools have different approaches to the teaching of GCSE Physical Education, so this resource has been designed to support your teaching without dictating teaching methods. You should teach in your own way, using audiovisual and ICT resources as appropriate. When students are required to make notes or conduct research, they should refer to the student book. Most note-taking can take place on sheets photocopied from the *Teacher Support Pack*.

Preparing and using the material

The revision guide sheets can be prepared in advance and presented to students in a file at the start of their course. Files can be conveniently stored in school and will be available for every lesson.

You may wish to provide each student with a plastic wallet in which to take home sheets for revision or research. Students can use the sheets for most note-taking within lessons. Their notes should be neat, with accurate diagrams to aid revision and understanding.

Activity worksheets could also be included in the file in advance of the course. However, you might prefer to select those activities most appropriate to your group and give the sheets out at the time that each activity is undertaken. These can be stored in students' files after completion.

Support for analysis of performance and practical elements of GCSE PE

The extensive range of worksheets relating to analysis of performance and coaching are ideal for teaching this important component of GCSE PE. They provide practical ideas and encourage the application of theory to sports performance. These materials are ideal for developing sports leadership, and many of the tasks provide material for classroom-based lessons which lead into a series of practical lessons based on the work completed – for example, 'Design a drill'.

How is revision supported?

At the end of their course, students will have created their own revision guide. Topics will be easily accessible in a style that actively aids learning. They will be revising their own words in a well-ordered and attractive format, illustrated throughout with high-quality diagrams.

Ideas for enhancing learning

Many new ideas are being disseminated through the KS3 strategy which can be applied equally to KS4. They include approaches to questioning and discussion which encourage participation by all students. The following are ideas which we have found to be effective.

'Traffic light' cards

Each student has a green, a yellow and a red card. During a review of previous work, the students respond to each question asked by the teacher by holding up a card. Green indicates that the holder is sure of the correct answer. Yellow suggests that the student has an idea of the answer, but is not sure that it is totally correct. A red card signifies that the holder does not know the answer.

The teacher receives instant feedback about the level of understanding within the group, can direct support where necessary and can encourage those with green cards held high to answer if appropriate.

'Thirty seconds'

When reviewing previous work at the start of a lesson, instead of asking for 'hands up', the teacher tells the group: 'You have 30 seconds to discuss possible answers with your neighbour. Then I will ask someone to report back.'

In this way the more reticent students have the opportunity to be selected to answer. Those who are unsure of the answer have the support of their neighbour and can try out possible answers in a 'safe' situation.

'Going for five'

Students are not allowed to put up their hands. Instead, the teacher says, 'Here is my question. Talk it through with the person next to you. You have two minutes to find five answers to it.'

This encourages reflective thinking and ensures that all students participate.

Examples:

- 'Think of five types of fitness and a test for each one.'
- 'Think of five different sports and a key type of fitness for each one.'
- 'Choose a sport and think of five aspects of fitness that contribute to good performance. Give reasons for each.'

Activities to develop thinking skills

The student book contains a number of activities that encourage students to think. Teachers can further develop thinking skills by using some of the ideas and examples described below. Some blank templates are provided for teacher use, but it is relatively easy to produce electronic versions of your own which can be modified for different topics.

'Odd one out'

Students are asked to highlight, or circle, the odd one out in a set of items. They must then state what the other three have in common.

This activity can be set by the teacher. Alternatively students can be asked to devise examples of their own.

Examples:

Pulmonary artery	Pulmonary vein	Aorta	Left atrium

200m	Marathon	Long jump	Javelin

A blank template for 'Odd one out' appears on page x.

Odd one out

Highlight, or circle, the odd one out in each set. Then state what the other three have in common in the space below.

_____

_____

_____

_____

_____

_____

_____

_____

_____

_____

_____

_____

'Fortune lines'

A series of cards are prepared containing words or statements. Students have to discuss possible sequences of events and place the cards in the correct order.

Example:

Each statement below refers to the experience of a 200m sprinter during a race. Place them in the order in which the sprinter experiences them.

Muscles work very hard without enough oxygen	Athlete breathes aerobically
Athlete breathes anaerobically	Muscles become tired
Oxygen debt is repaid	Athlete completes race and stops running
Lactic acid forms in the muscles	Athlete breathes aerobically

A blank template for 'Fortune lines' appears on page xii.

Fortune Lines/Keyword Cards

Keyword cards

These can either be prepared by the teacher beforehand, or written out by students and distributed to the class as a task. Class members are challenged to explain the word on the card they hold.

This is a useful revision tool, especially when students have to devise their own cards and are responsible for explaining the words that their classmates cannot.

Example: Keywords for principles of training

Specificity	Progression
Overload	Reversibility
Individual needs	Thresholds of training

The blank template for 'Fortune lines' on page xii can also be used for Keywords.

Memory mapping

Students are grouped into teams of four. Each team sends one person up to the front of the class to study a diagram for ten seconds. They then return to their group, who have to try to reproduce the diagram.

After a short period a second person has ten seconds to view the same diagram. After each student has had a turn, the teacher stops the activity and the students are asked to compare their versions of the diagram with the original.

Diagrams might include:

- a labelled cross-section of the heart
- a labelled diagram of the skeleton
- a labelled diagram of the muscular system
- a diagram of a complex skill development drill, including teaching points.

'Mind the gap!'

A list of information is projected on a computer screen. After a short period of observation the page is shown again with one word or phrase removed. The students have to identify the word that belongs in the gap.

This activity can also be completed by brainstorming words on to the whiteboard and then rubbing out words while members of the class close their eyes. It does work – with the right class! Be warned: some classes ask the teacher to take a turn...

Example:

Reducing the risk of injury

Types of injury	Causes of injury	Precautions
Fracture Hypothermia Sprain, concussion, strain, blisters	Violent impact Cold weather, overuse, environment, internal force	Protective equipment, following the rules, correct clothes, match competition, fitness, warm-up

Plenary sessions and debriefing

Debriefing is an essential part of teaching thinking lessons. Time should be set aside to discuss strategies with students. You might ask: 'What did you do? How did you do it? Why was that effective?'

It is by thinking, and talking about thinking, that learners start to gain an insight into their own learning, and that of others. This process is called metacognition.

Sometimes the discussion and review might be saved for the beginning of the next lesson. This will help the students to focus on how they are going to do something in a different, more effective, way.

This section contains additional material for two activities contained in the student book and for the activity on Worksheet 16.

Guilty or not guilty?

(Chapter 7: Diet, health and hygiene, page 143)

The latest information on the cases dealt with in this activity is as follows:

Alain Baxter
Found guilty: stripped of the Olympic Gold Medal, and banned from competition for three months by the International Ski Federation. The British Olympic Association invoked their byelaw and banned him from representing the UK in any subsequent Olympic Games. Baxter appealed, and the BOA's independent appeal panel found that he should be allowed to compete again, on the basis that the offence was minor and that 'significant mitigating circumstances existed in relation to the offence'.

Kelli White
At the time of publication the case is ongoing. The IAAF claim that modafinil is closely related to the banned stimulant ephedrine. White was cleared to compete in the 4 x 100-metre relay final but was not selected by the US team officials.

White was banned from competing in France between 1 January and 30 June 2003 after testing positive for triamcinolone at a Golden League meeting in Paris. This stimulant is not banned, but is illegal in France. White claimed to be using it to treat asthma.

Mark Bosnich
Received a nine-month suspension for improper conduct and a breach of FA doping control regulations. His appeal was dismissed and he was ordered to pay the Appeal Board's costs.

Blood circulation

(Chapter 9: The circulatory system, page 201)

Before running this activity, you will need to prepare labels representing the various parts of the circulatory system. See the templates on page 3.

Before the activity members of the group are chosen to represent the following:

● vena cava, right atrium, tricuspid valve, right ventricle, semiluna valve, pulmonary artery, lungs
● pulmonary veins, left atrium, mitral valve, left ventricle, aorta, arteries, arterioles, venules, veins.

Each member of the group has a card indicating which part of the circulatory system they represent.

Task 1

Students have five minutes to arrange themselves into the right order in a circle, starting with the vena cava. They must then decide whether red, blue, or red and blue blood flows through them.

Task 2

A student is chosen to represent a drop of blood and attempts to circulate through the system (each cardholder shows their card). In order to pass through each part of the system he/she must correctly answer one or more of the following questions:

- 'Are you red or blue blood?'
- 'Which part of the system have you just come from?'
- 'Are you carrying oxygen or carbon dioxide?'
- 'Where are you going next?'

Task 3

Task 2 can be repeated, but with the names of the various parts of the circulatory system hidden. The blood drops have to name the system part that they are visiting before they can proceed.

Chapter 9: The circulatory system   Pages 184–207

This sheet is for use in conjunction with the activity on page 201 of the student book. It needs to be photocopied onto card and cut into separate labels for distribution to students.

You may wish to make a reference copy on blue card.

Vena cava	Right atrium
Tricuspid valve	Right ventricle
Pulmonary artery	Semilunar valve
Lungs	Veins
	Venules

Edexcel Sport Examined Teacher Support Pack © Beashel, Sibson and Taylor, Nelson Thornes Ltd, 2004

This sheet is for use in conjunction with the Activity on page 201 of the student book. It needs to be photocopied onto card and cut into separate labels for distribution to students.

You may wish to make a reference copy on red card.

Arteries	Arterioles
Lungs	Aorta
Pulmonary vein	Left atrium
Mitral valve	Left ventricle
Semilunar valve	

Edexcel Sport Examined Teacher Support Pack © Beashel, Sibson and Taylor, Nelson Thornes Ltd, 2004

Statements for fitness classification

The statements in the grid below are for use in conjunction with the fitness classification activity on Worksheet 16. The sheet needs to be photocopied and cut into strips for distribution to students.

1 Interval training	**2** Ability to change the direction at speed
3 Ability to contract our muscles in one explosive act	**4** Maximum press-ups
5 Time for 50 metres	**6** Training using the movements of our sport at full speed
7 Ability of our muscles to carry out daily tasks. This includes muscular strength, muscular power and muscular endurance	**8** Stretching muscles and tendons beyond their normal range of movement
9 Developing skills through practice and training	**10** Focusing on important information
11 Ability to move body as quickly as possible	**12** Stimulus response computer test
13 Somatotyping	**14** Ability to maintain the right amount of muscle and fat
15 Bleep test	**16** Plyometrics
17 Diet and exercise	**18** Ability to work for long periods of time without becoming tired
19 Ability of muscles to perform our sport. Strength is a combination of muscular strength, muscular power and muscular endurance.	**20** Sit and Reach Test

Edexcel Sport Examined Teacher Support Pack © Beashel, Sibson and Taylor, Nelson Thornes Ltd, 2004

21 Using a dynamometer	**22** Ability to keep our equilibrium whether we are stationary or moving
23 Ability to carry out a series of movements smoothly and efficiently	**24** Training with heavy weights and low reps
25 Good coaching and regular practice	**26** Ability to respond to a stimulus quickly
27 Standing vertical jump	**28** Ability to use muscles to apply maximum force to an immovable object
29 Illinois Run	**30** Increased power
31 Ability to move the joints through their full range of movement	**32** Alternate Hand Wall Toss Test
33 Light weights with high repetition	**34** Ability to work our muscles very hard for a period of time.
35 Stork Stand	

Edexcel Sport Examined Teacher Support Pack © Beashel, Sibson and Taylor, Nelson Thornes Ltd, 2004

These simple-to-administer quizzes are designed to be set and marked verbally at the beginning of a lesson. Ideally, they should test student knowledge of topics covered in the previous lesson(s). A simple homework could be, 'Learn the topic for next week's ten-minute teaser'.

Students can mark their own, or their neighbour's answers. Marks can be collected verbally, and all students will be eager to beat their own, and each other's, previous score.

Questions

| Chapter 3 | 1. Health, fitness, exercise and performance |

What is:

a   Health?
b   Exercise?
c   Fitness?
d   Performance?
e   Cardiovascular fitness?
f   Muscular strength?
g   Flexibility?
h   Muscular endurance?
i   Body composition?
j   Name two ways to reduce fat and increase muscle in the body?

| Chapter 4 | 2. Skill-related fitness |

What is:

a   Agility?
b   Balance?
c   Co-ordination?
d   Health-related fitness?
e   Power?
f   Reaction time?
g   Skill-related fitness?
h   Speed?
i   Name one fitness factor that you would expect a high-jumper to possess.
j   Name one fitness factor that you would expect a fencer to possess.

Edexcel Sport Examined Teacher Support Pack © Beashel, Sibson and Taylor, Nelson Thornes Ltd, 2004

Chapters 3 and 4 3. Fitness testing

Name a test for each of the following:

a Cardiovascular fitness
b Muscular strength
c Muscular power
d Muscular endurance
e Flexibility
f Speed
g Agility
h Co-ordination
i Reaction time
j Balance.

Chapter 5 4. Principles of training

a List the five principles of training.
b List the four components of the FITT principles.
c List the four phases of a training session.
d What is meant by 'individual needs'?
e What is meant by 'thresholds of training'?
f How do we calculate MHR?
g What do the letters 'MHR' stand for?
h At what percentage of MHR is the aerobic threshold?
i At what percentage of MHR is the anaerobic threshold?
j Within which threshold would a marathon runner train?

Edexcel Sport Examined Teacher Support Pack © Beashel, Sibson and Taylor, Nelson Thornes Ltd, 2004

Chapter 6	5. Methods of training

Which type of training involves:*

a   Long runs?

b   Runs with sprints every now and then over varied terrain?

c   Periods of high intensity and recovery?

d   A number of different activities?

e   Working specific muscles to overcome resistance?

f   Leaping and bounding?

g   Which type of muscle contraction results in movement?

h   List the three phases of a training session.

i   What is meant by 'recovery rate'?

j   i   Name the waste product that forms in muscles when they work hard.

   ii   Describe its effect on muscles.

* This test can be extended by asking for an example of a sport or activity for which each type of training is suitable.

Chapter 7	6. Diet, health and hygiene

a   Which food type gives us quick energy?*

b   Which food type gives us energy slowly?*

c   Which food type aids growth and repair?*

d   What regulates chemical reactions in the body?

e   What other substances enable the body to work effectively?

f   What is useful although we cannot digest it?

g   What is essential for all of our systems?

h   What would happen to someone whose energy intake was lower than their energy output?

i   What two pieces of advice would you give to someone who wished to lose weight?

j   A marathon runner reduces activity for three days and eats lots of pasta before the race. What is this process called?

* This test can be extended by asking for an example of a foodstuff containing each food type.

Edexcel Sport Examined Teacher Support Pack © Beashel, Sibson and Taylor, Nelson Thornes Ltd, 2004

Chapter 7 7. Drugs and sport

What drug would lead to:

a Reduced lung capacity?

b Reduced co-ordination?

c Longer injury recovery time?

Which banned drug would lead to:

d Severe dehydration?

e Increased aggression?

f Hiding of symptoms of fatigue?

g Masking of pain?

h Name the technique that involves injecting blood.

i Which drug is banned in archery and shooting?

j Which drug leading to poor judgement is banned in motor sport and many games?

Chapter 8 8. Sports injuries

a What does RICE stand for?

b DRABC is a checklist. What does each letter stand for?

c Name two types of fracture.

d Name two types of joint injury.

e Which injury often follows unconsciousness?

f Name a common muscle injury.

g Which injury is caused by heat and lack of water?

h In which position should an unconscious person be placed?

i Name a common skin injury caused by overuse.

j Name a common joint injury caused by overuse and incorrect technique.

Edexcel Sport Examined Teacher Support Pack © Beashel, Sibson and Taylor, Nelson Thornes Ltd, 2004

Chapter 9 9. The circulatory system

a List the five functions of the circulatory system.

b List three differences between arteries and veins.

c In the simplest of terms, what does the heart do in the circulatory system?

d What name is given to an upper chamber of the heart?

e What name is given to a lower chamber of the heart?

f Which side of the heart contains oxygenated blood?

g Which vessel takes blood from the heart to the lungs?

h Which vein carries oxygenated blood?

i Name two valves within the heart.

j Which chambers send blood away from the heart, the upper or lower? (Use the correct name.)

Chapter 9 10. Blood

a What are the three main functions of blood in athletic performance?

b What forms 55% of the volume of blood?

c What name is given to the component of blood that carries oxygen?

d Where is the oxygen-carrying component found?

e Which component deals with disease and damage to the body?

f Which component helps to produce clotting?

g What is blood pressure?

h Why do we measure blood pressure?

i List five things that affect blood pressure.

j What name is given to the condition of having high blood pressure?

Edexcel Sport Examined Teacher Support Pack © Beashel, Sibson and Taylor, Nelson Thornes Ltd, 2004

Chapter 10 11. The respiratory system

a What anatomical name is given to the windpipe?

b What name is given to the parts of the lungs where gaseous exchange takes place?

c When breathing in, does the diaphragm contract or relax?

d What do the ribs do when breathing in?

e What do the ribs do when breathing out?

f The respiratory centre of the brain monitors the levels of a gas in your body and tells you when to breathe. Which gas does it monitor?

g What name is given to the amount of air that we normally breathe in and out?

h What name is given to the largest amount of air that can be forced out of the lungs in one breath?

i What name is given to the process where oxygen is used to release the energy in glucose within our body cells?

j What substance is produced in the muscles when respiration takes place anaerobically?

Chapter 11 12. The skeleton

a List the five functions of the skeleton.

b What name is given to the process of bone development?

c Name the thin protective coating around each long bone.

d Which type of bone is a carpal?

e Which type of bone is the femur?

f Which type of bone is the sternum?

g Which type of bone might you find in the face?

h Why does drinking milk help bones to develop?

i Of which substance are the bones of an embryo made?

j What name is given to the area where the arms attach to the body?

Edexcel Sport Examined Teacher Support Pack © Beashel, Sibson and Taylor, Nelson Thornes Ltd, 2004

Chapter 11 13. Name the bones

a What is the anatomical name for the thigh bone?
b What is the anatomical name for the finger and toe bones?
c Name the bone of the upper arm.
d Which bones are located in the back of your hand between the wrist and fingers?
e Name the two bones of the forearm.
f What name is given to the bone in the centre of your chest.
g Name the two bones between your knee and ankle.
h What is the anatomical name for the collarbone?
i Name the flat bone in the upper back (you have two of them).
j Name the bone which is located within the quadriceps tendon.

Chapter 12 14. Joints, tendons and ligaments

a Where will you find a ball and socket joint?
b Of which type of joint is the elbow an example?
c Name the two bones which form the shoulder joint.
d Give an example of a pivot joint.
e Name the role of tendons at joints.
f What role do ligaments have at joints?
g Which type of movement is this? (Demonstrate bringing your arm towards and across your body.)
h Which type of movement is this? (Straighten your leg, or stand up from your chair.)
i Which type of movement is this? (Flex your biceps.)
j Which type of movement does a diver perform when executing a somersault?

Edexcel Sport Examined Teacher Support Pack © Beashel, Sibson and Taylor, Nelson Thornes Ltd, 2004

Chapter 13 15. Muscles and muscle action

a Name the three types of muscle.

b Give an example of an antagonistic pair of muscles.

c Name the two types of muscle fibre.

d Which type of muscle fibre uses oxygen?

e What is muscle tone?

f Give two reasons why good posture is important.

g Name a sport in which a high level of fast twitch fibres is needed.

h Name a sport in which a high level of slow twitch fibres is needed.

i When flexing the elbow, which muscle is the prime mover?

j When flexing the knee which muscle is the antagonist?

Chapter 13 16. Name the muscles

a Which muscle extends the knee?

b Which muscles abduct and extend the hip?

c Which muscle surrounds and moves the shoulder?

d Which muscle in the back extends and adducts the shoulder?

e Which muscles in the chest move the arm and shoulder?

f Which muscle is the fixator for the shoulder and neck?

g Which muscles flex the knee joint?

h Which muscle flexes the elbow?

i Name the antagonist to the muscle in the previous question.

j Which muscle group forms the 'six pack'?

Note: If you prefer, you can simply point to each muscle in your own body and ask for the correct name

Edexcel Sport Examined Teacher Support Pack © Beashel, Sibson and Taylor, Nelson Thornes Ltd, 2004

Watch a group of your classmates playing a small-sided game, for example, indoor hockey or netball. Try to decide who is the most effective player. Now explain why his or her performance is so effective. Is the player fitter? Faster-thinking? Harder-working? More skilful?

Player	Marks (out of 10)					
	Speed	Skill	Thinking	Effort	Fitness	Overall
1						
2						
3						
4						
5						
6						
7						
8						
9						
10						

Who is the most effective player? _____
_____
_____

In which areas does he/she score most highly? _____
_____
_____

Which aspect of play has the biggest impact on effectiveness? _____
_____
_____

In which areas do players need to improve to become more effective? _____
_____
_____
_____

Edexcel Sport Examined Teacher Support Pack © Beashel, Sibson and Taylor, Nelson Thornes Ltd, 2004

Are there any special terms in your chosen sport? Think about equipment, rules, techniques and strategies. Produce a list of terms on small cards. Then pass the cards amongst your class. Each person has to explain the term to the rest of the class. If they don't know the answer you will have to make sure that you can explain it.

Use this template to cut out individual cards.

 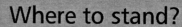

Choose a technique from a sport of your choice and consider where you should stand to observe it. Is it best to stay in one place? Do you need to observe from a number of different angles to get an overall picture – for example, from the side, the front or from behind? Are you better placed at ground level, or should you observe from above?

Sport _____   **Technique** _____

1   Draw a simple diagram to show where you would stand to observe the technique.

2   Explain how your position(s) will help you to observe and analyse the technique.

_____

_____

_____

_____

_____

_____

_____

_____

_____

_____

_____

_____

_____

_____

Edexcel Sport Examined Teacher Support Pack © Beashel, Sibson and Taylor, Nelson Thornes Ltd, 2004

  Observing a technique in action

Select a technique from a sport that requires a feeder. Write down a list of the parts of the technique that you wish to observe. Decide who is to feed, and give precise instructions to the feeder. Then observe the technique in action and analyse the performance.

Sport _____ **Technique** _____

Use the table below to organise your thoughts before, during and after the activity

What will I observe?	_____
Instructions to feeder	_____
What is good about the technique as currently performed	_____
What can be improved?	_____

Edexcel Sport Examined Teacher Support Pack © Beashel, Sibson and Taylor, Nelson Thornes Ltd, 2004

Observe a group member playing a competitive game and assess his or her performance. Focus your observation on planning, performance and evaluation. Discuss your findings with the player and suggest ways to improve.

Give examples of each and summarise at the end.

Player _____   **Sport** _____   **Date** _____

Planning

Does the player seem to know what he/she is trying to do? Is there a pattern to his/her play?

Always ☐   Sometimes ☐   Never ☐

Example(s): _____

_____

Performance

Is the player's technique good enough to carry out his/her ideas with accuracy and consistency?

Always ☐   Sometimes ☐   Never ☐

Example(s): _____

_____

Evaluation

Is the player learning to improve his/her level of performance from experiences within the game?

Always ☐   Sometimes ☐   Never ☐

Example(s): _____

_____

Summary

Is the player effective?

Always ☐   Sometimes ☐   Never ☐

Include positive comments and areas for improvement.

_____

_____

_____

_____

_____

_____

Edexcel Sport Examined Teacher Support Pack © Beashel, Sibson and Taylor, Nelson Thornes Ltd, 2004

Choose a sport and decide on the data to be gathered in order to analyse the performance of a team. This may be the number of successful passes, tackles, attacks, etc. Have at least two observers for each team. Observe a team for a period of time and note everything that happens on a checklist.

The checklist below is designed for football or hockey, but it can be adapted to suit other sports. It could also be adapted to record observations of individual players or particular aspects of the game – e.g. 'Ball played into team/opposition penalty area'.

Sport	Period of observation (mins)	Tally total
Aspects observed	*Record each incident with a tally mark*	
Pass completed		
Possession lost		
Successful tackle		
Unsuccessful tackle		
Shot off-target		
Shot on-target		

Using the data

Describe the performance of the team/player based on the data you have gathered.

_____

_____

_____

_____

_____

_____

Which aspects of the game need to be improved?

_____

_____

_____

_____

_____

_____

Edexcel Sport Examined Teacher Support Pack © Beashel, Sibson and Taylor, Nelson Thornes Ltd, 2004

Analysing a strategy

Consider this example from football, then decide how you could observe and gather data in order to advise the managers.

Mickey and Johanne are experienced managers of teams in a local football league.

- Mickey believes that his team will be more successful in getting the ball into the opposition penalty area if his goalkeeper always plays the ball out to a full back to restart play. He thinks that his players will keep possession and create scoring opportunities for his strikers in the opposition penalty area.

- Johanne has told his goalkeeper to always kick the ball as far up the pitch as possible. He thinks that this will lead to more scoring opportunities in the opposition penalty area.

Neither manager has any facts to back up their beliefs.

Can you find some facts to support one of the managers?

You could gather data by observing a number of live football matches on TV. You will need to decide what to look for, and create a rota of observers, so that each match has at least two people watching the entire 90 minutes. Once you have collected enough information you will know which is the best strategy.

You might wish to send the results to your local club to help their manager!

Edexcel Sport Examined Teacher Support Pack © Beashel, Sibson and Taylor, Nelson Thornes Ltd, 2004

Which is the Perfect Model?

Look at the two athletes in the photographs on page 2 of *Edexcel Sport Examined*. One demonstrates the Perfect Model. The other is an intermediate performer.

Working with a partner, discuss the strengths and weaknesses of each performer. Then decide what feedback you would give to the intermediate performer to help improve performance. Remember to look for good points too.

Athlete 1

Good points

_____

_____

_____

_____

Weaknesses

_____

_____

_____

_____

Feedback

_____

_____

_____

_____

Athlete 2

Good points

_____

_____

_____

_____

Weaknesses

_____

_____

_____

_____

Feedback

_____

_____

_____

Edexcel Sport Examined Teacher Support Pack © Beashel, Sibson and Taylor, Nelson Thornes Ltd, 2004

Consider the following situations and, in groups, make suggestions for strategies and tactics for improving individual or team performance.

You must explain to the whole group how you think your tactic or strategy will make a difference.

1 Your basketball team is losing heavily at half time. One player of average height but excellent all-round court movement has scored most of the opposition's points. Your zone defence has been unable to cope with him.

Strategies	Tactics

2 Your hockey team is winning 1–0 with 15 minutes remaining in the match. The opposition are playing almost entirely in your half. Your defenders are tired and keep hitting the ball away, but the opposition regain possession very quickly.

Strategies	Tactics

3 You are a middle-distance runner. Both you and your rival have personal best times of 5 minutes for the mile (4 laps of the track). You plan to race at 75 seconds per lap and then outsprint your rival to the finish. You begin the race and stay at the shoulder of the leader. However, after the first lap your rival speeds up to a pace of 65 seconds per lap.

Strategies	Tactics

Edexcel Sport Examined Teacher Support Pack © Beashel, Sibson and Taylor, Nelson Thornes Ltd, 2004

Use the grid below to plan, design and evaluate a training drill for your chosen sport.

Sport _____

What is the drill trying to teach/develop/improve?

How many players are involved?

What do they each do (e.g. feeder, doer, coach, ball collector etc.)?

What equipment is needed (e.g. bibs, balls, cones, goals, rackets, nets, posts, etc.)?

Edexcel Sport Examined Teacher Support Pack © Beashel, Sibson and Taylor, Nelson Thornes Ltd, 2004

What does the drill look like? Write a key in this column.	Draw a diagram here

Edexcel Sport Examined Teacher Support Pack © Beashel, Sibson and Taylor, Nelson Thornes Ltd, 2004

What instructions will I have to give to explain the drill?

(How many times do the players repeat the drill?)

What happens after the first player has completed the drill?

How do the players know if they have been successful?

How well did the drill work? How might I improve it next time?

Edexcel Sport Examined Teacher Support Pack © Beashel, Sibson and Taylor, Nelson Thornes Ltd, 2004

Choose a technique or skill from the sport of your choice.

Describe an example of each type of practice for your chosen sport.

Sport _____

Unopposed drill

_____
_____
_____
_____
_____

Passive opposition drill

_____
_____
_____
_____
_____

Active opposition drill

_____
_____
_____
_____
_____

Pressure training drill

_____
_____
_____
_____
_____

Try out each type of practice above with your group.

You may find that some of your group cope well with them all. Others' performance may deteriorate as the pressure increases.

27

Do you know how many officials are required to control a game or event in your chosen sport? Research the answer and complete a checklist with details of each official and the roles they have.

Sport _____

Title of official	Role

Edexcel Sport Examined Teacher Support Pack © Beashel, Sibson and Taylor, Nelson Thornes Ltd, 2004

There are many reasons why people take part in sport. These reasons will be linked to their particular lifestyle and the influence of home, school and friends.

Read the following pen pictures and discuss why you think each individual takes part in their chosen sport. Note your ideas in the box below each character.

John is a 26-year-old accountant and works in the City. His job is very demanding; he works long hours most days of the week, tends to eat out a lot and goes to the pub regularly. He does go to the gym three lunchtimes a week and works out on both weights and aerobic machines. He also tries to have a run or a cycle ride each weekend.

Nisha is a freelance graphic designer who works from home. She is single and in her late twenties and has little contact with the outside world during her working week. She tends to eat a lot, has problems controlling her weight and worries about her appearance. As a student she enjoyed dance and has recently joined a modern dance group which meets twice a week.

29

Martin is 17 years old and has returned to college after failing most of his recent exams. He gets frustrated with his lack of progress and loses his temper quite easily. He has always enjoyed sport without making the school teams, but his PE teacher recommended on leaving school, that he joined the local rugby club. He now trains twice a week with the club and plays a match every weekend. He has also started serious weight training at a local gym.

Eighteen-year-old Ellie is quiet and shy and took little part in sport and PE at school. Through a friend at work, she met a parascending group who eventually persuaded her to try the sport. To her surprise, not only did she enjoy the thrills of the sport but realised that she was quite good. She is now secretary of the group, taking part every weekend and has also developed a growing interest in paragliding.

Other reasons for taking part in sport

Think of your own experiences – are they different/similar to the reasons listed above? Make notes and discuss them in your group.

After discussing all the reasons for taking part in sport, try to sort them into categories under the headings Social, Physical and Mental.

In small groups, look at the following pen pictures and decide what in the lifestyles of these people makes them healthy and unhealthy. Make brief notes below each description.

Phil is a 45-year-old married male with a wife and two young children. He has been unemployed for two years and is often depressed. His wife has a part-time job but does not earn very much. He watches a lot of television and likes fast food and beer. He supports his local football team but his regular exercise is limited to walking his children to and from school each day. He is overweight and would find running for a bus quite stressful even though he is a non-smoker.

Healthy	Unhealthy

Sylvia is a 63-year-old widow who lives by herself but has a cat. She walks half a mile to the shops and back each day and each weekend she joins the local Ramblers on one of their walks. She likes the occasional glass of wine but watches her weight carefully. She smokes 20 cigarettes a day. She enjoys being with her many grandchildren and rarely needs to visit her doctor.

Healthy	Unhealthy

John is 16 and spends most of his spare time on his computer, often working until the early hours. He not only plays games on it but also uses the internet to keep up to date with his music and his friends. At school he takes part in archery and weight lifting but does not participate in any lunchtime or after-school sporting activities. His mother ensures he eats sensibly at home and prepares sandwiches and fruit for his lunch every day.

Healthy	Unhealthy

31

Sarah, now 26, is confined to a wheelchair following a road accident five years ago. She was an outstanding hockey player before her accident and plays wheelchair basketball for her county. This involves regular training sessions including fitness work in the gym. She drives her own specially adapted car and has a boyfriend who plays rugby for a local team.

Discuss your answers about the lifestyles and try to agree answers to the following questions.

Healthy	Unhealthy

Which of the people has the healthiest lifestyle? _____

Why is this?

_____
_____
_____
_____
_____
_____

Who has the least healthy lifestyle? _____

_____

What advice would you give to this person?

_____
_____
_____
_____
_____
_____

Edexcel Sport Examined Teacher Support Pack © Beashel, Sibson and Taylor, Nelson Thornes Ltd, 2004

Work in threes to complete the tests below, then enter the scores for your group on the results grid on Worksheet 15b.

Read the instructions carefully to make sure you perform the task correctly.

Circuit	
Tennis ball pick-up	Place 3 tennis balls on floor 2 metres away. Run, pick up first ball and return both feet behind starting line. Repeat with second and third ball. Finish as quickly as you can. Record time taken to complete test.
Balancing ball	Extend arm at right angles to the ground, fist clenched, back of hand facing upwards. Place volleyball on back of hand and time how long it can be balanced up to a maximum of 60 seconds. Arm may be moved but not feet.
The pinch	Have a partner pinch a fold of fat on back of your upper arm, halfway between the elbow and the tip of the shoulder. Measure fold in cms.
Two-ball juggle	Hold two tennis balls in your preferred hand. Juggle them up to 10 times without dropping either ball. Score one point for each catch up to maximum of 10.
Shoulder raise	Lie face-down on floor with arms stretched out in front. Hold a metre rule with your hands shoulder-width apart. Raise arms as high as possible, keeping chin on the ground at all times and rule parallel to the floor. Hold highest position for 3 seconds. A partner measures the height reached.
Grip test	Squeeze a hand grip dynamometer as hard as possible with one hand.
Standing broad jump	Start with feet comfortably apart and toes immediately behind start line. Then bend knees and jump forward as far as possible. Measure distance from your rear heel back to the start line. You are allowed two attempts.
Press-ups	Complete as many press-ups as possible in 60 seconds. Girls can perform press-ups from the kneeling position.
Metre rule drop	Have a partner hold a metre rule so that side edge is between your thumb and index finger at a point 30 cm from end. When your partner releases rule, catch it before it slips through your thumb and finger. Do not move your hand lower to catch ruler. Record how far rule has fallen.
Double heel click	With feet apart, jump up and tap heels together twice before you hit ground. You must land with your feet at least 10 cm apart. Make three attempts.
Shuttle run	Complete a 10-metre shuttle run as many times as possible over a two-minute period.

Edexcel Sport Examined Teacher Support Pack © Beashel, Sibson and Taylor, Nelson Thornes Ltd, 2004

Enter the scores for your group on the grid below

Activity	Name:	Name:	Name:	Name:
Tennis ball pick-up				
Balancing ball				
The pinch				
Two-ball juggle				
Shoulder raise				
Grip test				
Standing broad jump				
Press-ups				
Metre rule drop				
Double heel click				
Shuttle run				

Each group reports back on its results. Once all results have been collected:

1 Calculate the average score for each activity for your class.
2 Note the highest score achieved in your class.
3 Note the type of fitness that you think each exercise measures.
4 Give an example of a sport for which each type of fitness is important.

Activity	Average score for class	Highest score for class	Type of fitness measured	Sport for which type of fitness is important
Tennis ball pick-up				
Balancing ball				
The pinch				
Two-ball juggle				
Shoulder raise				
Grip test				
Standing broad jump				
Press-ups				
Metre rule drop				
Double heel click				
Shuttle run				

Discuss the results within your class. How does the average score compare with the highest score? Is your class fitter in some types of fitness than in others? Why is this?

Edexcel Sport Examined Teacher Support Pack © Beashel, Sibson and Taylor, Nelson Thornes Ltd, 2004

1 In your group, carefully read through and discuss the statements provided on slips by your teacher.

2 Sort the statements into three categories:
   – definitions of a fitness factor
   – types of fitness test
   – ways to improve a fitness factor.

3 Complete the table below by writing the number of each statement in the appropriate box.

	Definition of fitness factor	Fitness test	Way to improve fitness factor
Agility			
Balance			
Body composition			
Co-ordination			
Flexibility			
Muscular strength			
Muscular power			
Muscular endurance			
Reaction time			
Speed			
Cardiovascular fitness			

Edexcel Sport Examined Teacher Support Pack © Beashel, Sibson and Taylor, Nelson Thornes Ltd, 2004

Look at the pictures below.

In which picture(s) can you see examples of:

Fitness factor	Picture
Good dynamic balance	
High level of cardiovascular fitness	
Extreme flexibility	
Appropriate body composition	
Good muscular strength	
High level of power	
Extensive muscular endurance	
Exceptional speed	
Considerable agility	
Skilful co-ordination	
Fast reaction time	

Edexcel Sport Examined Teacher Support Pack © Beashel, Sibson and Taylor, Nelson Thornes Ltd, 2004

Look at the fitness requirements of your chosen sport.

1 Mark them on the chart.
2 Look at your levels of fitness by carrying out the tests on the charts below.
3 Grade yourself using tables in *Edexcel Sport Examined*.
4 Mark your fitness levels, in a different colour, on the chart.
5 Look at the chart to see the areas in which you need to train harder to improve your performance. Use this information when preparing your PEP.

Sport _____

PERSONAL FITNESS LEVEL

TEST	High	Above average	Average	Below average	Low	FITNESS REQUIREMENTS OF THE SPORT
Stork stand						Balance
Alternate hand wall toss						Co-ordination
Sit and reach						Flexibility
Illinois agility run						Agility
NCF addominal curl						Muscular endurance
Hand grip dynamometer						Maximum strength
Standing board jump						Muscular power
Cooper 12 minute run						Stamina

37

Edexcel Sport Examined Teacher Support Pack © Beashel, Sibson and Taylor, Nelson Thornes Ltd, 2004

Explore the effectiveness of training by carrying out the following experiment.

1   Arrange yourselves into three groups containing approximately equal numbers of boys and girls.
2   Each person in each group attempts to juggle three tennis balls, using both hands. Count the number of successful catches. Select the best score from three attempts.
3   Calculate the average score for each group and the average score for boys and girls and record the score on the table below.
4   Now train for 20 minutes.
    –   Group A practises juggling with 3 tennis balls for 20 minutes
    –   Group B practises bouncing a tennis ball continuously on the ground, for 20 minutes
    –   Group C practises juggling with 3 tissues or scarves for 20 minutes.
5   Repeat the juggling task and record the results.

	GROUP A			GROUP B			GROUP C		
	Group Average	Boys Average	Girls Average	Group Average	Boys Average	Girls Average	Group Average	Boys Average	Girls Average
Attempt 1									
Attempt 2									

Discuss the following questions using the data from the tests to support your answers.

1   What sort of practice is most likely to improve your juggling skills?

_____
_____
_____
_____

2   Is this true for both boys and girls?

Yes ☐   No ☐

3   Is practising bouncing a tennis ball more likely to improve your juggling skills than practising with tissues?

Yes ☐   No ☐

4   Do you think your answers would apply to other sporting skills?

Yes ☐   No ☐

5   Does slowing down the skill (e.g. using the tissues/scarves) when practising improve learning?

Yes ☐   No ☐

In small groups, examine the following training programmes and decide how far each programme has been based on the principles of training. Complete the summary sheet and be prepared to discuss your finding with the whole class.

Programme 1: Six-week programme for Sharon, a cross-country runner

	Monday	Tuesday	Wednesday	Thursday	Friday	Saturday	Sunday
Week 1	Ten-mile run	Gym work, concentrating on upper body strength	Fartlek	Track work, 400-metre repetitions x 10	Rest day	Race	30-mins swimming continuous lengths
Next 5 weeks	No change	Increase weights gradually	Increase total distance run	Reduce rest time between repetitions	Rest day	Race	No change

Programme 2: Six-week programme for Errol, a badminton player

	Monday	Tuesday	Wednesday	Thursday	Friday	Saturday	Sunday
Week 1	Skill practice for 1 hour	Endurance training on the court – 1 hour	Light weights in gym (high reps)	Gym work, 30-mins run, 20 mins bike, 20 mins rowing	Match practice	Stretching and plyometrics	League game
Next 5 weeks	No change	No change	Increase speed and reps	Increase work rate	No change	No change	League game

Programme 3: Six-week programme for Mandy, a footballer

	Monday	Tuesday	Wednesday	Thursday	Friday	Saturday	Sunday
Week 1	5-a-side matches	Power lifting in gym	Match	Rest day	10-mile run	Match	Rest day
Next 5 weeks	No change	Heavier weights	No change	No change	No change	No change	No change

Programme 4: Six-week programme for Ahmed, a swimmer

	Monday	Tuesday	Wednesday	Thursday	Friday	Saturday	Sunday
Week 1	100-metre repetitions – various strokes x 20	200-metre repetitions – various strokes x 10	1 hour technique improvement including turns	2 miles continuous – fast	1 hour technique improvement including turns	Competition	5 miles continuous lengths
Next 5 weeks	Reduce time for both reps and recovery	Reduce time for both reps and recovery	No change	No change	No change	No change	No change

Edexcel Sport Examined Teacher Support Pack © Beashel, Sibson and Taylor, Nelson Thornes Ltd, 2004

Summary sheet

	Sharon	Errol	Mandy	Ahmed
Specificity	Good/Bad Why?	Good/Bad Why?	Good/Bad Why?	Good/Bad Why?
Progression	Good/Bad Why?	Good/Bad Why?	Good/Bad Why?	Good/Bad Why?
Overload	Good/Bad Why?	Good/Bad Why?	Good/Bad Why?	Good/Bad Why?
Reversibility	Good/Bad Why?	Good/Bad Why?	Good/Bad Why?	Good/Bad Why?
Tedium	Good/Bad Why?	Good/Bad Why?	Good/Bad Why?	Good/Bad Why?
Overall suitability	Good/Bad Why?	Good/Bad Why?	Good/Bad Why?	Good/Bad Why?

Edexcel Sport Examined Teacher Support Pack © Beashel, Sibson and Taylor, Nelson Thornes Ltd, 2004

Consider the following training sessions for Floella, Jim, Janice and Mustafa.

Calculate their individual aerobic and anaerobic thresholds and decide in which training zone they are working.

1   Floella is a 26-year-old racing cyclist and during a sprint training session she tries to maintain her heart rate at 155 beats per minute.

Aerobic threshold	Anaerobic threshold	Active training zone

2   Jim, who is 30 years old, is doing a cross-country run and has maintained a heart rate of 158 for the last 15 minutes.

Aerobic threshold	Anaerobic threshold	Active training zone

3   Janice is 18 years old and is doing interval training. Today's training session involves her completing ten 60-metre sprints with her heart rate raised to 170 beats per minute.

Aerobic threshold	Anaerobic threshold	Active training zone

4   Mustafa, who is 47 years old, swims regularly and keeps his heart rate above 105 throughout his swim.

Aerobic threshold	Anaerobic threshold	Active training zone

Edexcel Sport Examined Teacher Support Pack © Beashel, Sibson and Taylor, Nelson Thornes Ltd, 2004

Prepare a training schedule for your chosen sport. List the key aspects of each training session in each of the periods.

At the top of the table enter the months which fall into each period for your chosen sport. For football these would be:

- Off-season: June, July
- Pre-season: July
- Peak season: August to May.

Sport _____

Peak season	Off-season	Pre-season
Months	Months	Months

Prepare a training session specific to your chosen sport. Be sure to consider periodisation and match what you include in the session with the training period in which it is to fit (pre-, peak or off-season).

Include enough detail to allow someone else to lead the session if necessary. You may need to use this sheet for planning and then produce a separate, detailed, piece of work.

Sport _____   **Training period** _____

Warm-up

Main activity

Warm-down

43

Working in pairs:

1 Record your resting pulse rate for 15 seconds and record it on the table below.
2 Complete a warm-up then run 400 metres as fast as possible.
3 Ask your partner to record your pulse for 15 seconds at 30-second intervals for 5 minutes. Record the results on the table.
4 Repeat the activity with the roles reversed.

	Student 1 _____		Student 2 _____	
	Pulse rate (15 seconds)	Heart rate (beats per minute)	Pulse rate (15 seconds)	Heart rate (beats per minute)
Resting				
30 secs				
1 min.				
1 min. 30 secs				
2 min.				
2 min. 30 secs				
3 min.				
3 min. 30 secs				
4 min.				
4 min. 30 secs				
5 min.				

5 Plot both sets of heart rates on the graph below.

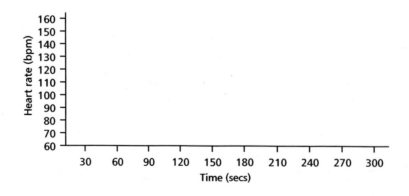

Who is fitter – you or your partner?

Edexcel Sport Examined Teacher Support Pack © Beashel, Sibson and Taylor, Nelson Thornes Ltd, 2004

All the sportspeople shown above are performing well in their chosen sports. They have trained hard, but their body build and their lifestyle also help them.

Look at the pictures and discuss the following questions:

What is it about the body type (shape and size) of each person that helps them to excel at their sport? _____.

_____

_____

_____

_____

How will their training differ? _____

_____

_____

_____

_____

Which person is likely to eat more food each day? _____

_____

_____

_____

_____

Would you expect their diets to be different? In what ways? _____

_____

_____

_____

_____

45

Edexcel Sport Examined Teacher Support Pack © Beashel, Sibson and Taylor, Nelson Thornes Ltd, 2004

1 Interview a parent, grandparent or friend.
2 List the amount of food and drink that they consume in a typical day.
3 Write down the amount and type of activity they have had during that day.

Food and drink	Activity

Write a summary about the effect that their diet and activity pattern will have on their weight.

_____

_____

_____

_____

_____

_____

What advice would you offer them about this?

_____

_____

_____

_____

_____

_____

Edexcel Sport Examined Teacher Support Pack © Beashel, Sibson and Taylor, Nelson Thornes Ltd, 2004

Select two products, a sports energy drink and a snack bar, and investigate their ingredients.

Compare them and give advice about their likely effects.

Name of food product	Name of drink product
Description:	Description:
Kj per 100g/ml	Kj per 100g/ml
Carbohydrate content per 100g/ml	Carbohydrate content per 100g/ml
Other key ingredients	Other key ingredients
Claimed effect (e.g. 'boosts energy')	Claimed effect
Conclusions and advice	Conclusions and advice

Edexcel Sport Examined Teacher Support Pack © Beashel, Sibson and Taylor, Nelson Thornes Ltd, 2004

Imagine that you are a member of the UK sport drug-testing team.

Using the table below, list all the currently banned and restricted types of drug, and the sports in which you would be likely to encounter each type of drug.

Banned or restricted drug	Sports

Using the internet, carry out a search to find out whether the drugs on your list have been found in the sports that you have indicated.

Edexcel Sport Examined Teacher Support Pack © Beashel, Sibson and Taylor, Nelson Thornes Ltd, 2004

List the number of hours you spend asleep or resting during a typical week. Add a comment if you wish.

Analyse your sleep and rest pattern and explain the effect that it is likely to have on your sporting performance.

Day	Hours of rest	Hours of sleep	Comment
Monday			
Tuesday			
Wednesday			
Thursday			
Friday			
Saturday			
Sunday			

How will my rest and sleep pattern affect my sporting performance?

_____

_____

_____

_____

_____

How might I modify my lifestyle to improve performance?

_____

_____

_____

_____

_____

Look at the following cartoons of sporting activities and complete the grid listing all the potential safety hazards.

Sport	Safety hazards		
	Equipment	Clothing	Other
Trampolining			
Climbing			
Gymnastics			
Rugby			
Cricket			
Basketball			

All sports have rules designed to minimise the risk of injury to participants. For example in football girls are not allowed to play against boys after the age of 11, players who raise their feet too high close to an opponent are penalised and all players must wear shin guards.

Choose three sports and, for each one, write down three rules designed to prevent accident or injury.

Sport _____

Rule 1 _____.

Rule 2 _____.

Rule 3 _____.

Sport _____

Rule 1 _____.

Rule 2 _____.

Rule 3 _____.

Sport _____

Rule 1 _____.

Rule 2 _____.

Rule 3 _____.

Edexcel Sport Examined Teacher Support Pack © Beashel, Sibson and Taylor, Nelson Thornes Ltd, 2004

Imagine that you are organising a sporting tournament.

Describe the basic organisation, including the age and gender of teams, the number of teams and the number of pitches/courts or other facilities that will be needed.

Complete a risk assessment listing potential hazards and the safety measures that you will need to take to avoid accidents or injuries.

Description of tournament:

_____

_____

_____

_____

_____

_____

_____

_____

_____

Hazards	Risk factor (1–5)	Safety measures (actions/instructions)

Edexcel Sport Examined Teacher Support Pack © Beashel, Sibson and Taylor, Nelson Thornes Ltd, 2004

Look at the pictures below and answer the questions.

Type of injury? _____

Likely cause of injury? _____

How avoided? _____

Type of injury? _____

Likely cause of injury? _____

How avoided? _____

Type of injury? _____

Likely cause of injury? _____

How avoided? _____

Edexcel Sport Examined Teacher Support Pack © Beashel, Sibson and Taylor, Nelson Thornes Ltd, 2004

The simplest way to measure the efficiency of our circulatory system is to record our heart rate and pulse.

We can easily take a pulse at two specific locations – in the neck at the carotid artery and in our wrist on the radial artery.

1 Practise counting the number of pulses over 15 seconds. Use your fingers and not your thumb. Try it at both the neck and wrist. Multiply your 15-second count by 4 to get your heart rate in beats per minute.

2 Practise locating your carotid and radial pulses quickly.

3 While sitting down at rest, practise counting the pulse of your partner using both the neck and wrist locations.

4 One of you now walks at a brisk pace for one minute. Immediately after walking, the non-active partner measures the other's pulse for the first 15 seconds and records it in beats per minute.

5 Repeat the exercise with roles reversed.

6 The first partner now jogs for three minutes at a slow pace. Repeat the pulse-taking and swap over.

7 You both now play a game – say, basketball – for 10–15 minutes. Repeat the pulse-taking.

8 Your partner sprints for a total of 20 seconds. Repeat the pulse-taking and swap over.

9 You both warm down for three minutes. Repeat the pulse-taking and swap over.

10 Plot your results and those of your partner on the table and on the graph on Worksheet 34b. Remember, you should not join the points on the graph as the data you have collected is not continuous. Give reasons to explain your results.

Edexcel Sport Examined Teacher Support Pack © Beashel, Sibson and Taylor, Nelson Thornes Ltd, 2004

Time period	Activity	Heart rate (beats per minute)
	Rest	
1 minute	Walk	
3 minutes	Jog	
10–15 minutes	Play game	
20 seconds	Sprint	
3 minutes	Warm down	

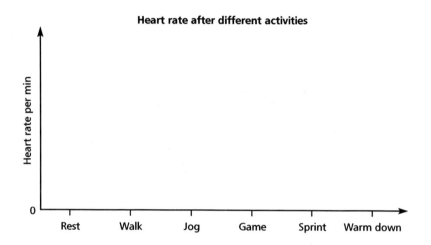

Explain your findings.

_____

_____

_____

_____

_____

_____

_____

_____

_____

_____

_____

_____

1 Depending on the equipment available, practise taking your partner's blood pressure when he or she is sitting down and resting. Record both the systolic and diastolic measures.

2 One of you now walks at a brisk pace for one minute. Immediately after walking, the non-active partner measures the other's blood pressure and records it.

3 Repeat the exercise with roles reversed.

4 The first partner now jogs for three minutes at a slow pace. Repeat the blood pressure recording and swap over.

5 You both now play a game of, for example, basketball for 10–15 minutes. Repeat the blood pressure recording.

6 Your partner sprints for a total of 20 seconds. Repeat the blood pressure recording and swap over.

7 You both warm down for three minutes. Repeat the blood pressure recording and swap over.

8 Plot your results and those of your partner as a dual bar chart. Do not join the points plotted as the data you have collected is not continuous. Give reasons to explain your results.

Recording blood pressure (contd)

Time period	Activity	Systolic blood	Diastolic blood
	Rest		
1 minute	Walk		
3 minutes	Jog		
10–15 minutes	Play game		
20 seconds	Sprint		
3 minutes	Warm down		

Explain your findings.

_____

_____

_____

_____

_____

_____

_____

_____

_____

_____

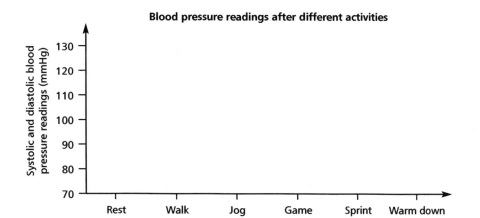

Blood pressure readings after different activities

57

Matt and Dwayne are 23-year-old middle-distance runners. When they are resting, their breathing rates are both the same: 16 breaths a minute. However, Matt is able to get much more oxygen to his working muscles and therefore produces much faster times than Dwayne. Read the descriptions below and try to think of three reasons to explain the difference in their times.

Matt is 1.6 metres tall, weighs 61 kg and is of ectomorphic body type. He works as a bricklayer and is able to vary his working hours to fit in with his training. He is a member of his local athletics club and trains three times a week on the track. He has a very experienced coach who bases his training on high-quality track work involving interval training.

Dwayne is 1.9 metres tall and weighs 85 kg. He is a call-centre operator and works long regular hours (9 am–6 pm) five days a week. He is a member of his local athletics club but trains on his own with some advice from his father, who is a former athlete. His training consists mainly of long runs and a body building session in the gym once a week.

The following questions may help your discussions:

● Body size and lung size are closely related. Will this have any effect on cardiovascular endurance?

● Can body weight or body type have an effect on cardiovascular endurance?

● What is the importance of aerobic fitness and anaerobic fitness for running the 1,500 metres?

● Do you think the time Matt and Dwayne have given to training and the way they have trained will affect their performances at 1,500 metres?

Edexcel Sport Examined Teacher Support Pack © Beashel, Sibson and Taylor, Nelson Thornes Ltd, 2004

Notes

_____

_____

_____

_____

_____

_____

_____

Reasons for the differences in times

1 _____

_____

_____

_____

_____

_____

_____

2 _____

_____

_____

_____

_____

_____

_____

3 _____

_____

_____

_____

_____

_____

Discuss the answers to these questions in your group and choose someone to report back to the whole class.

Edexcel Sport Examined Teacher Support Pack © Beashel, Sibson and Taylor, Nelson Thornes Ltd, 2004

Your breathing rate tells you how much air, and therefore oxygen, is entering your lungs and will be passed into the blood and taken to the tissues.

You can measure this by placing one hand across your chest and counting the number of times your chest rises in 15 seconds. Multiplying by 4 gives you your breathing rate per minute.

Look at the table below.

Perform the activities listed in the table and check your breathing immediately after the time period ends.

Complete the table.

Activity	Time period	Breathing rate (breaths per minute)
Rest		
Walk	1 minute	
Jog	3 minutes	
Play game (e.g. basketball	10–15 minutes	
Sprint	20 seconds	
Warm down	3 minutes	

Now plot the results on the graph below.

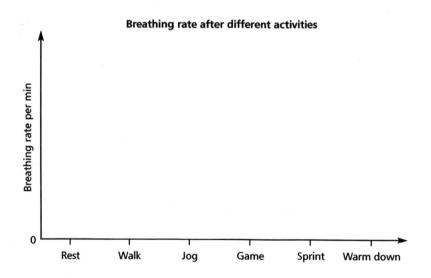

Breathing rate after different activities

Answer the questions on Worksheet 37b

Questions

What do you notice about changes in your breathing rate?

_____

_____

_____

How do you explain this effect?

_____

_____

_____

Calculate the mean breathing rate for your class in each time period and plot the results on the table below.

Activity	Time period	Breathing rate (breaths per minute)
Rest		
Walk	1 minute	
Jog	3 minutes	
Play game (e.g. basketball	10–15 minutes	
Sprint	20 seconds	
Warm down	3 minutes	

Compare the mean for the class with the breathing rates of individuals.

Note and discuss any significant differences in breathing rates within your class.

_____

_____

_____

How do you explain these differences?

_____

_____

_____

Edexcel Sport Examined Teacher Support Pack © Beashel, Sibson and Taylor, Nelson Thornes Ltd, 2004

1 Working with a partner, attempt each of the four movements listed in the tables below. Take it in turns to observe each other. You might wish to use a video camera to record and play back the movement. Each movement has two phases: preparation and the action itself.

2 Fill in the table by noting down the joints, type of movement and muscles used.

	Description of movement	Joints used	Type of movement	Muscles used (Note if contraction is eccentric or concentric)
Kicking a stationary ball (preparation)	Drawing the leg back	Hip Knee	Extension Flexion	Gluteals Hamstrings
Kicking a stationary ball (action)	Kicking the ball			
Shooting for goal in netball (preparation)				
Shooting for goal in netball (action)				
Playing a pull shot in cricket (preparation)				
Playing a pull shot in cricket (action)				
Doing a straddle jump from the floor or trampoline (preparation)				
Doing a straddle jump from the floor or trampoline (action)				

Edexcel Sport Examined Teacher Support Pack © Beashel, Sibson and Taylor, Nelson Thornes Ltd, 2004

 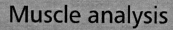
Working in pairs, carry out the activities listed below while your partner identifies which major muscle groups are being used. Examples of muscle groups include: upper back, lower back, upper arm, lower arm, chest, shoulder, stomach.

Begin lying flat on your back, then complete each action when instructed to do so by your partner.

Action	Major muscle groups being used
Move to sit-up position	
Stand up	
Raise hands above head	
Raise one knee and hold for five seconds	
Complete one press-up	
From standing position, jump as high as possible	

Edexcel Sport Examined Teacher Support Pack © Beashel, Sibson and Taylor, Nelson Thornes Ltd, 2004

From the following description of a movement, try to work out what action is being performed.

The body is in a standing position with the arms by the side. The deltoids contract to raise the arm so that it is parallel to the ground. The muscles of the fingers are flexed to grip an object. The biceps contract slowly and then the triceps contract powerfully and the fingers extend as the object is released.

Write your own movement description below and see if your partner can work out what action is taking place. Be prepared to demonstrate some or all of the action if necessary. You may need to refine your description following discussion.

Description of action

_____

_____

_____

_____

_____

_____

_____

_____

_____

_____

_____

Revised description of action

_____

_____

_____

_____

_____

_____

_____

_____

_____

_____

Edexcel Sport Examined Teacher Support Pack © Beashel, Sibson and Taylor, Nelson Thornes Ltd, 2004

Complete the table by giving examples of the qualities promoted by sport and physical activity.

Quality promoted	Examples from sport
Co-operation	
Competition	
Physical challenge	
Aesthetic appreciation	

List ways in which physical activity:

• helps people to achieve mental well-being

_____

_____

• to achieve physical well-being

_____

_____

• to achieve social well-being.

_____

_____

What is stress-related illness?

_____

_____

Give an example of a stress-related illness.

_____

_____

Explain how physical activity can relieve stress.

_____

_____

Sport and friendship

Give an example of how physical activity encourages friendships and social mixing.

_____

_____

_____

_____

_____

Edexcel Sport Examined Teacher Support Pack © Beashel, Sibson and Taylor, Nelson Thornes Ltd, 2004

It is important to know the correct definition of each of the following terms.
Refer to *Edexcel Sport Examined* for help.

Health and fitness are not the same thing.

Health is _____

_____

Fitness is _____

_____

Give examples of health-related fitness for everyday life.

Cardiovascular fitness _____

_____

Muscular strength _____

_____

Muscular endurance _____

_____

Flexibility _____

_____

Body composition _____

_____

When training and playing sport we use the terms exercise and performance.

Performance is _____

Exercise is _____

Give an example of exercise done only to improve fitness.

_____

_____

_____

Edexcel Sport Examined Teacher Support Pack © Beashel, Sibson and Taylor, Nelson Thornes Ltd, 2004

1 Define each aspect of fitness, using definitions from *Edexcel Sport Examined*.
2 Explain, with an example, the importance of each one to physical activity.

Outline a training activity to improve each type of fitness.

Definitions	Importance to physical activity (with example)
Cardiovascular fitness is	
Improved through	
Maximum strength is	
Improved through	
Muscular endurance is	
Improved through	
Flexibility is	
Improved through	
Body composition is	
Improved through	

Edexcel Sport Examined Teacher Support Pack © Beashel, Sibson and Taylor, Nelson Thornes Ltd, 2004

1 Define each of the five factors of fitness, using definitions from *Edexcel Sport Examined*.

2 Explain, with an example, the importance of each one to physical activity.

3 Outline a training activity to improve each type of fitness.

Definitions	Importance to physical activity (with example)
Agility is	
Improved through	
Balance is	
Improved through	
Co-ordination is	
Improved through	
Power is	
Improved through	
Reaction is	
Improved through	
Speed is	
Improved through	

Edexcel Sport Examined Teacher Support Pack © Beashel, Sibson and Taylor, Nelson Thornes Ltd, 2004

We should apply the SPORT principles to all training programmes.

Define each of the principles.

Specificity

_____

Progression

_____

Overload

_____

Reversibility

_____

Tedium

_____

Meeting individual needs

When we apply the specificity principle we train for a specific sport and also for our own individual needs. Give an example to explain this.

_____

_____

_____

_____

_____

What are the FITT principles?

We can use the FITT principles when planning fitness programmes.

Write what each letter stands for below.

F _ _ _ _ _ _ _ _ _ = how often we train

I _ _ _ _ _ _ _ _ _ = how hard we train

T _ _ _ = how long we train

T _ _ _ = what kind of training we do.

Edexcel Sport Examined Teacher Support Pack © Beashel, Sibson and Taylor, Nelson Thornes Ltd, 2004

By calculating our Maximum Heart Rate (MHR) we can work out our own thresholds for both aerobic and anaerobic training.

For boys, MHR = 220 – your age

For girls, MHR = 226 – your age

Fill in the missing words

My MHR = __ __ __ – _____ (my age) = ____ beats per minute.

To train my aerobic system I should work at __ __ % of MHR.

To train my anaerobic system I should work at __ __ % of MHR.

The required heart rates for various training effects for a 16-year-old

Label the diagram to indicate the training zones for each type of fitness.

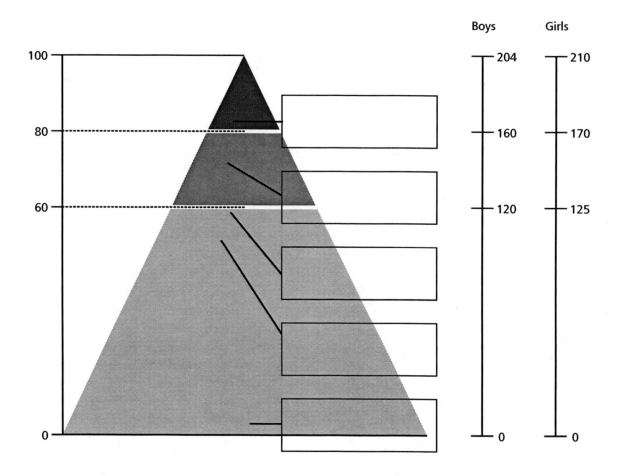

Edexcel Sport Examined Teacher Support Pack © Beashel, Sibson and Taylor, Nelson Thornes Ltd, 2004

Muscle contraction

Chapter 6: Methods of training   Pages 96–127

Our muscles can work in different ways according to the actions being performed.

Complete the sentences.

Isotonic contraction results in _____ .

It can be concentric or eccentric.

Concentric contraction takes place when _____

_____ .

An example in sport is

_____

_____

Eccentric contraction takes place when _____

_____ .

An example in sport is

_____

_____ .

Isometric contraction results in _____ but

_____ .

An example in sport is

_____

_____ .

71

Edexcel Sport Examined Teacher Support Pack © Beashel, Sibson and Taylor, Nelson Thornes Ltd, 2004

Training methods

Define training, using the definition in *Edexcel Sport Examined*.

Training is _____

There are many different training methods. They are all based on the different ways our body adapts to regular exercise.

Below and on Revision Guide 8b you will find descriptions of eight different training methods.

Write the name of each, then give examples of sports or activities for which the training method is suitable.

1 _ _ _ _ _ _ _ _

'Speed play' is the English term for this method. It involves varying the pace at which we walk, run or cycle and the type of terrain we travel over. It is good for improving stamina and recovery rate.

This form of training is suitable for: _____

2 _ _ _ _ _ _ _ _ _ _

This involves exercise without rest intervals. There are two types:

- Long/slow distance involves whole-body activity between 60–80% MHR and is good for general conditioning work and improving stamina.
- High intensity work at 85–95% MHR improves speed and endurance.

Long/slow distance is suitable for: _____

High intensity is suitable for: _____

3 _ _ _ _ _ _ _ _

This involves alternating periods of work with periods of rest. Training sessions can be longer because the rest periods allow us to recover. We can vary:

- the time or distance of each period of work
- the amount of effort (intensity)
- the length of time we rest
- the type of activity we do when resting
- the number of work and recovery periods in each session.

This form of training is suitable for: _____

4 _ _ _ _ _ _ _ _ _ _ _ _

This form of training uses methods associated with one sport or physical activity to improve fitness for another sport. It adds variety to a training programme and can prevent overuse injuries.

This form of training is suitable for: _____

Edexcel Sport Examined Teacher Support Pack © Beashel, Sibson and Taylor, Nelson Thornes Ltd, 2004

5 _ _ _ _ _ _ _ _ _ _ _ _ _ _ _ _

The most popular form of resistance training. It can be adapted for any sport.

SPORT principles should be followed when using this method.

Reps are the number of times we repeat an exercise without resting.

Sets are the number of reps done in succession; for example, one set = 10 reps.

Suitable for: _____

6 _ _ _ _ _ _ _ _ _ _ _

This form of training involves stretching a muscle before it contracts and using bounds, hops, jumps, leaps, skips, ricochets, swings and twists.

It is best to do this on grass or on mats in the gym to avoid joint injury.

Suitable for: _____

7 _ _ _ _ _ _ _ _ _ _ _ _ _ _

We perform a series of selected exercises or activities in a given sequence. It can be designed to improve aerobic or anaerobic fitness. We can make it more difficult by:

- increasing the number of stations
- increasing the time spent at each station
- increasing the number of reps at each station
- increasing the number of complete sets of exercises we complete.

Suitable for: _____

8 _ _ _ _ _ _ _ _ _ _ _ _ _ _ _ _ _

This method improves the range of movement at a joint. We can use a variety of stretching exercises involving:

- static stretching – holding a position for 10 seconds
- passive stretching – using a partner to apply force
- active stretching – repeated stretches for 20 seconds
- PNF stretching – stretching immediately after contraction.

Suitable for: _____

Edexcel Sport Examined Teacher Support Pack © Beashel, Sibson and Taylor, Nelson Thornes Ltd, 2004

An individual training session should consist of three phases.

Complete the table below by naming the phases of a training session in the top boxes and describing the activities of each phase below.

Phase 1	Phase 2	Phase 3

The main activity of a training session can include three types of training activity.

List each below and give examples of each.

Type of main activity	Examples
1	
2	
3	

Edexcel Sport Examined Teacher Support Pack © Beashel, Sibson and Taylor, Nelson Thornes Ltd, 2004

Chapter 6: Methods of training   Pages 96–127

List the effects of exercise under the different headings below.

What are the immediate effects of exercise on bones, joints and muscles?

- _____
- _____
- _____
- _____
- _____
- _____

What are the effects of regular training and exercise on bones, joints and muscles?

- _____
- _____
- _____
- _____
- _____
- _____
- _____
- _____

What are the long-term benefits of exercise on bones, joints and muscles?

- _____
- _____
- _____
- _____
- _____

Edexcel Sport Examined Teacher Support Pack © Beashel, Sibson and Taylor, Nelson Thornes Ltd, 2004

List the effects of exercise under the different headings below.

What are the immediate effects of exercise on the cardiovascular system?

- _____
- _____
- _____
- _____
- _____

What are the effects of regular training and exercise on the cardiovascular system?

- _____
- _____
- _____
- _____
- _____

What are the long-term benefits of exercise on the cardiovascular system?

- _____
- _____
- _____
- _____
- _____
- _____
- _____
- _____

Edexcel Sport Examined Teacher Support Pack © Beashel, Sibson and Taylor, Nelson Thornes Ltd, 2004

Chapter 6: Methods of training   Pages 96–127

List the effects of exercise under the different headings below.

What are the immediate effects of exercise on the respiratory system?

- _____
- _____
- _____
- _____

What are the effects of regular training and exercise on the respiratory system?

- _____
- _____
- _____
- _____

What are the long-term benefits of exercise on the respiratory system?

- _____
- _____
- _____
- _____
- _____

Edexcel Sport Examined Teacher Support Pack © Beashel, Sibson and Taylor, Nelson Thornes Ltd, 2004

 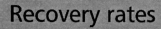
Chapter 6: Methods of training   Pages 96–127

Complete the sentences to explain recovery rates

Whenever we exercise, our heart rate _ _ _ _ _ _ _ _ _ _ to supply more _ _ _ _ _ _ _
to our working muscles. As a result our pulse rate increases from its _ _ _ _ _ _ _ _ level
to a higher level depending on how hard we work. We can measure levels of fitness by working
out how long a person's pulse rate takes to return to _ _ _ _ _ _ _ after exercise. This is
called the _ _ _ _ _ _ _ _ _ rate. During the recovery period the body deals with the
_ _ _ _ _ _ _ _ _ _ _ _ _. This is achieved by breathing _ _ _ _ _ _ _, transporting
more _ _ _ _ _ _ _ from the lungs and removing the _ _ _ _ _ _ _ _ _ _ _ _.

The recovery process is helped by gentle _ _ _ _ _ _ _ _ exercise immediately after the
vigorous activity. This aids the removal of _ _ _ _ _ _ _ _ _ _ _ _ _, reduces the possible
effect of _ _ _ _ _ _ _ _ _ _ _ _ _ _ _ _ and _ _ _ _ _ _ _ _ _ recovery time.

Use the data in the table below to plot a graph.

		Heart rate recorded at 30-second intervals after activity								
	0 secs	30 secs	60 secs	90 secs	120 secs	150 secs	180 secs	210 secs	240 secs
Luke	154	148	140	126	112	90	84	72	66
Jake	162	154	150	142	130	116	106	90	84

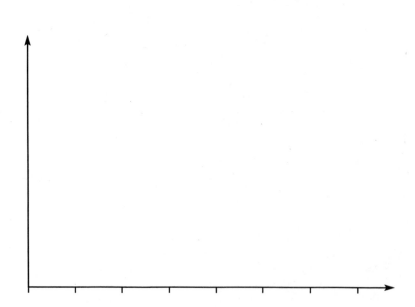

Which athlete is fitter, Luke or Jake?

 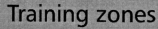

Chapter 6: Methods of training   Pages 96–127

1 Label the graph below to indicate:

   – time
   – heart rate
   – aerobic threshold
   – anaerobic threshold.

2 Using the graph, plot the typical heart rate of an athlete working within his or her aerobic training zone.

Edexcel Sport Examined Teacher Support Pack © Beashel, Sibson and Taylor, Nelson Thornes Ltd, 2004

 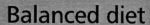

A balanced diet consists of seven essential components: carbohydrates, fats, proteins, vitamins, minerals, fibre and water.

Complete the chart below by listing foods containing carbohydrates, fats and proteins and describing their importance in exercise and activity.

Food type		Found in	Importance for exercise
Carbohydrates	Sugar		
	Starch		
Fats	Saturated		
	Unsaturated		
Proteins			

Chapter 7: Diet, health and training   Pages 128–156

A balanced diet consists of seven essential components: carbohydrates, fats, proteins, vitamins, minerals, fibre and water.

Complete the chart below by listing foods containing vitamins, minerals, fibre and water and describing their importance in exercise and activity.

Food type		Contained in	Importance for exercise
Vitamins	A		
	B		
	C		
	D		
	E		
Minerals	Calcium		
	Iron		
	Magnesium		
	Potassium		
	Sodium		
Fibre			
Water			

Edexcel Sport Examined Teacher Support Pack © Beashel, Sibson and Taylor, Nelson Thornes Ltd, 2004

Chapter 7: Diet, health and training   Pages 128–156

We need energy to make our bodies work. There are two main purposes for energy. Describe each below.

Basic Metabolic Rate (BMR) _____

_____

Physical Activity Level (PAL) _____

_____

How is energy measured?

There are two common measurements of energy. List them below.

_____

_____

The energy equation

Our diet, weight and energy needs are linked together. Many diets and schemes attempt to complicate the simple facts about weight gain and weight loss.

Label each of the diagrams below.

Write a sentence to explain each diagram.

_____
_____
_____
_____

_____
_____
_____
_____

_____
_____
_____

Edexcel Sport Examined Teacher Support Pack © Beashel, Sibson and Taylor, Nelson Thornes Ltd, 2004

SPORT examined — Revision Guide 17 — Body weight and performance

Chapter 7: Diet, health and training   Pages 128–156

Complete the sentences below.

What is overweight?

Being overweight simply means __ _ _ _ _ _ _ _ _ _ _ _ _ _ _ _ _ _
_ _ _ _ _ _ _ _ _. This is normally based on the standard height/weight tables. Being
overweight is not a problem if it is _ _ _ _ _ _ _ _ _ _ of _ _ _ _ _ _ _ _ _ _ _.

What is overfat?

If we are overfat our body _ _ _ _ _ _ _ _ _ _ _ _ _ contains too much _ _ _.
A male body should contain about _ _ _ _ _ _. A female body should contain
about _ _ _ _ _ _.

What is obesity?

If our weight is over _ _ _ more than the _ _ _ _ _ _ _ _ _ weight for our height, we
are _ _ _ _ _ _. Obesity often leads to _ _ _ _ _ _, _ _ _ _ _ _ _ _ _ _ _ _ _ and
other _ _ _ _ _ _ problems.

Being slightly overweight can affect sports performance and it _ _ _ _ _ _ _ _ _ _ the
_ _ _ _ _ _ _ _ _ _ _ _ _ _ _ _ _ _ _ _ _.

What are anorexia and bulimia?

Undereating can lead to loss of weight and this will also affect performance.

Anorexia sufferers do not allow themselves to _ _ _ and they often think they
are _ _ _ _ _ _ _ _ _ _ _.

Bulimia sufferers eat a lot of food, but _ _ _ _ _ _ _ _ _ _ _. They usually do this
by _ _ _ _ _ _ _ _ _.

Both conditions lead to _ _ _ _ _ _ _ _ _ _ _ _ _ _ _ _ _ _ _ _ _
_ _ _ _ _ _ _ _ _ _.

These are medical conditions. Sufferers need urgent medical help.

83

Edexcel Sport Examined Teacher Support Pack © Beashel, Sibson and Taylor, Nelson Thornes Ltd, 2004

Chapter 7: Diet, health and training   Pages 128–156

Together with body size (height compared to weight) and body composition (amount of fat), our body type indicates the kind of sports in which we might be successful. There are three main body types. We are all part endomorph, mesomorph and ectomorph.

1 Label the diagrams of these extreme body types.

2 Write a short description of each one.

3 List sports for which each type is well suited.

This body type is an:	This body type is a:	This body type is an:
_____	_____	_____
Characteristics include:	Characteristics include:	Characteristics include:
_____	_____	_____
_____	_____	_____
_____	_____	_____
_____	_____	_____
_____	_____	_____
_____	_____	_____
Suitable sports include:	Suitable sports include:	Suitable sports include:
_____	_____	_____
_____	_____	_____
_____	_____	_____
_____	_____	_____

Chapter 7: Diet, health and training   Pages 128–156

Complete the following sentences.

When we work hard the energy we use comes from stores of _ _ _ _ _ _ _ _ _. This is made from _ _ _ _ _ _ _ _ _ _ _ _ _ _ _ _ and _ _ _ _. To have enough energy for endurance events we must eat _ _ _ _ _ _ _ _ _ _ _ _ _ _ _ _ _ _ _ _. We call this _ _ _ _ _ _ _ _ _ _ _ _ _ _ _ _ _ _ _ _ _ _. We do this by _ _ _ _ _ _ _ _ our level of exercise for _ _ _ _ _ _ _ _ _ _ before competition. At the same time we _ _ _ _ _ _ _ _ the amount of _ _ _ _ _ _ _ _ _ _ _ _ _ in our _ _ _ _.

Carbohydrates or fats?

Our bodies use carbohydrates, in the form of glycogen, and fats to produce energy. The mixture used depends on the length and intensity of your activity.

Complete these examples:

When resting we use mainly _ _ _ _ _.

On a long walk we will 'burn' mainly _ _ _.

If we start jogging we will use _ _ _ _ _ _ _ _ _.

When jogging for a few hours we will use _ _ _ _ _.

When sprinting our muscles use _ _ _ _ _ _ _ _ _.

Endurance training teaches our body to use more _ _ _ during exercise. This helps our limited supplies of _ _ _ _ _ _ _ _ _ _ _ _ _ _ to last longer.

_ _ _ _ _ _ _ _ are only rarely used as an energy supply. This happens when all other _ _ _ _ _ _ _ _ _ _ _ _ _ _ have been used.

How should we eat for sport?

List the advice you might give to a sportsperson

Eating before exercise _____

_____

_____

Eating during exercise _____

_____

Eating after exercise _____

_____

_____

Edexcel Sport Examined Teacher Support Pack © Beashel, Sibson and Taylor, Nelson Thornes Ltd, 2004

There are many different social drugs. Each has a different effect.

Describe the effects of each drug on sporting performance.

Drug	Effect on sporting performance
Alcohol	
Amphetamines	
Caffeine	
Cannabis	
Cocaine	
Ecstasy	
LSD	
Nicotine (tobacco)	

Edexcel Sport Examined Teacher Support Pack © Beashel, Sibson and Taylor, Nelson Thornes Ltd, 2004

The classes of drugs shown on the diagram below are banned in many sports. Write a brief description of the effect each type of drug would have on an athlete, together with the major dangers of each.

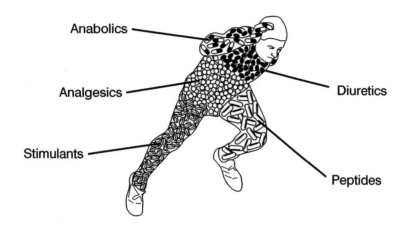

Anabolics _____

_____

Analgesics _____

_____

Stimulants _____

_____

Diuretics _____

_____

Peptides _____

_____

Blood doping does not involve the use of drugs. Describe this doping method and its effects.

_____

_____

_____

_____

Edexcel Sport Examined Teacher Support Pack © Beashel, Sibson and Taylor, Nelson Thornes Ltd, 2004

Complete the sentence, then fill in the table by describing how and why we should keep each area of the body healthy and clean.

Hygiene means

_____

_____

Area of the body	How and why it should be kept clean and healthy
Skin	
Nails	
Hair	
Teeth	
Feet	

Make notes about each of these foot conditions

Athlete's foot	What is it?	How is it treated?
Verrucæ	What are they	How are they treated?

There are many ways in which players can reduce the risk of injury.

Explain each of the methods in the table and give an example from sport.

Way to reduce risk		Explanation and example
Rules of the game		
Correct clothing		
Correct footwear		
Protective clothing		
Specialist equipment		
Balanced competition	Grading by: weight	
	age	
	gender	
	skill level	
Warm-up		
Cool-down		

Edexcel Sport Examined Teacher Support Pack © Beashel, Sibson and Taylor, Nelson Thornes Ltd, 2004

In order to avoid sports injuries, we need to know what they are and why they happen.

Complete the diagram below by adding notes to describe each type of injury.

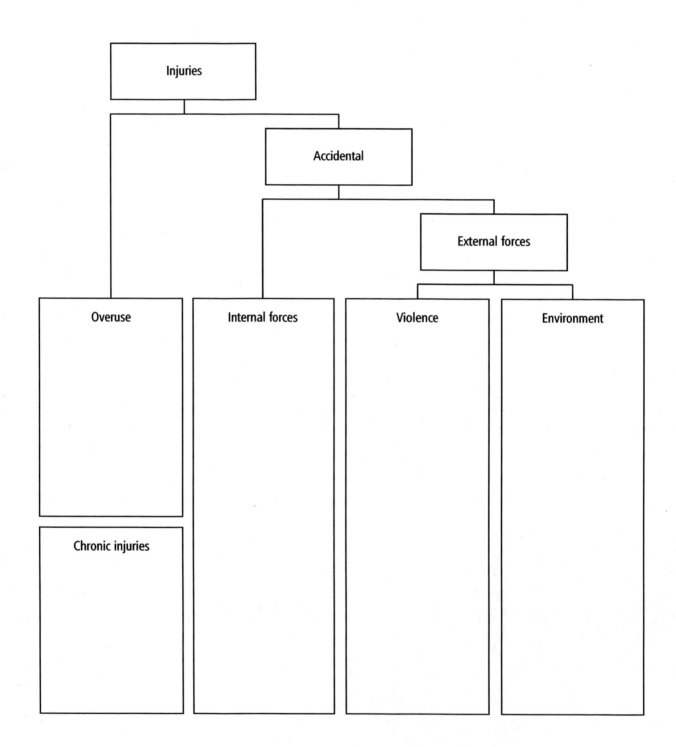

Edexcel Sport Examined Teacher Support Pack © Beashel, Sibson and Taylor, Nelson Thornes Ltd, 2004

A fracture is a break in a bone. There are two types of fracture.

Write a description of each type of fracture.

In a simple (closed) fracture

_____ .

In a compound (open) fracture

_____ .

Label the diagrams showing each type of fracture.

Type of fracture _____

_____

Type of fracture _____

_____

What are stress fractures?

Stress fractures are small cracks in a bone, often caused by too much running on hard surfaces.

Signs of a stress fracture are: _____

_____

_____

In the case of a stress fracture we should: _____

_____

_____

Dislocation

A dislocation means that a bone at a joint is forced out of its normal range of movement. This often causes further damage.

Answer the following questions.

What else might be damaged when a bone is dislocated?

_____

What might cause a dislocation?

_____

How should dislocations be treated?

_____

Cartilage injury

The two cartilages act as _ _ _ _ _ _   _ _ _ _ _ _ _ _ _ _ between the bones of the knee joint. They can be torn when the joint is twisted or pulled in an unusual way, for example during a _ _ _ _ _ _ _ in _ _ _ _ _ _ _ _ _ _.

We would need to seek _ _ _ _ _ _ _ _ _   _ _ _ _ _ _ _ if this occurred.

Sprains

A sprain happens when we over-stretch or tear a _ _ _ _ _ _ _ _ _ _.

A sprain can be caused by a _ _ _ _ _ _ _ or a sudden _ _ _ _ _ _ _ _, for example, a _ _ _ _ _ _ _ _ _ _ _   _ _ _ _ _ _.

We must use the _ _ _ _ _ treatment to treat sprains.

If the injury is severe we should treat it as a _ _ _ _ _ _ _ _ _ _.

Tennis elbow

'Tennis elbow' and 'golf elbow' are examples of _ _ _ _ _ _ _ _   _ _ _ _ _ _ _ _ _ _ _.

We can often tell that a bone or joint injury has happened by identifying the telltale signs.

List nine signs of bone or joint injury that can be checked for immediately.

1 _____

2 _____

3 _____

4 _____

5 _____

6 _____

7 _____

8 _____

9 _____

Some injuries are hard to diagnose. Describe an early sign of a break that you might recognise when you first see the casualty.

_____

_____

_____

Describe the four actions that you would take in treating a bone or joint injury

1 _____

2 _____

3 _____

4 _____

Edexcel Sport Examined Teacher Support Pack © Beashel, Sibson and Taylor, Nelson Thornes Ltd, 2004

Strains

A strain happens when we stretch or tear a _ _ _ _ _ _ or a _ _ _ _ _ _ _,
for example, a _ _ _ _ _ _ _ _ _ _ _ _ _.

We must use the _ _ _ _ treatment to treat strains.

Treatment of minor soft tissue injuries

We should deal with minor soft tissue injuries quickly and carefully, or they could become more serious.

Write down the treatments in the spaces provided below.

Skin damage	Treatment
Cuts	
Grazes	
Blisters	
Bruises	

Edexcel Sport Examined Teacher Support Pack © Beashel, Sibson and Taylor, Nelson Thornes Ltd, 2004

RICE is a checklist to follow when treating most soft tissue injuries. We should treat the injuries as soon as possible after they occur.

Write down what each letter stands for and explain the meaning of each word.
Then:

1 describe the action you would take at each stage
2 give the reason.

R stands for __ __ __ __.

Action _____

_____

Reason _____

_____

I stands for __ __ __.

Action _____

_____

Reason _____

_____

C stands for __ __ __ __ __ __ __ __ __ __ __.

Action _____

_____

Reason _____

_____

E stands for __ __ __ __ __ __ __ __ __.

Action _____

_____

Reason _____

_____

Edexcel Sport Examined Teacher Support Pack © Beashel, Sibson and Taylor, Nelson Thornes Ltd, 2004

In an emergency we should always get medical help if possible, but there may be times when we have to deal with a serious injury ourselves. It is important that our first treatment is correct, so we must not panic.

Remembering the checklist DRABC ('Doctor ABC') will help us focus on the key points.

Complete the flow diagram to help you to remember the correct order of action.

Danger

....

↓

Response

....

↓

Ask

....

Conscious	Unconscious

Airway

•	• ....
•	• ....
•	• ....
•	• ....
•	• ....

Breathing

Breathing	Not breathing
•	• ....
•	• ....
•	• ....
	• ....
	• ....

Circulation

Pulse present	No pulse
•	• ....
•	• ....
•	• ....

Complete the table below.

Condition	What is this condition?	What are the signs?	How do we treat it?
Concussion			
Shock			
Serious bleeding			
Hypothermia			
Heat exhaustion (caused by dehydration)			
Heatstroke			

Edexcel Sport Examined Teacher Support Pack © Beashel, Sibson and Taylor, Nelson Thornes Ltd, 2004

Complete the sentences.

Always use the recovery position for an unconscious person who is _ _ _ _ _ _ _ _ _ _ _.

We may need to alter the position slightly if the person has injuries, but we can roll him or her towards us and into the basic recovery position as follows:

- _____
- _____
- _____
- _____

Look at the diagram

List the key features of the recovery position

- _____
- _____
- _____
- _____

Remember to:

- _____
- _____

Edexcel Sport Examined Teacher Support Pack © Beashel, Sibson and Taylor, Nelson Thornes Ltd, 2004

The circulatory system is sometimes also called the cardiovascular system. Cardiovascular is another word used to describe the heart, blood vessels and blood.

List the functions of the circulatory system.

It takes _____

It removes _____

It carries _____

It maintains _____

It prevents _____

An overview of the circulatory system

1 Label the general plan of the circulatory system.
2 Colour the arteries red and the veins blue (except the pulmonary arteries and veins).

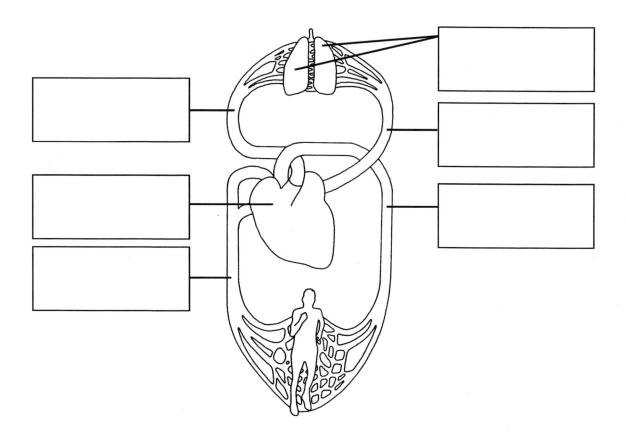

Edexcel Sport Examined Teacher Support Pack © Beashel, Sibson and Taylor, Nelson Thornes Ltd, 2004

Chapter 9: The circulatory system   Pages 184–207

1 Label the diagram.
2 Colour the heart blue to show deoxygenated blood and red to show oxygenated blood.

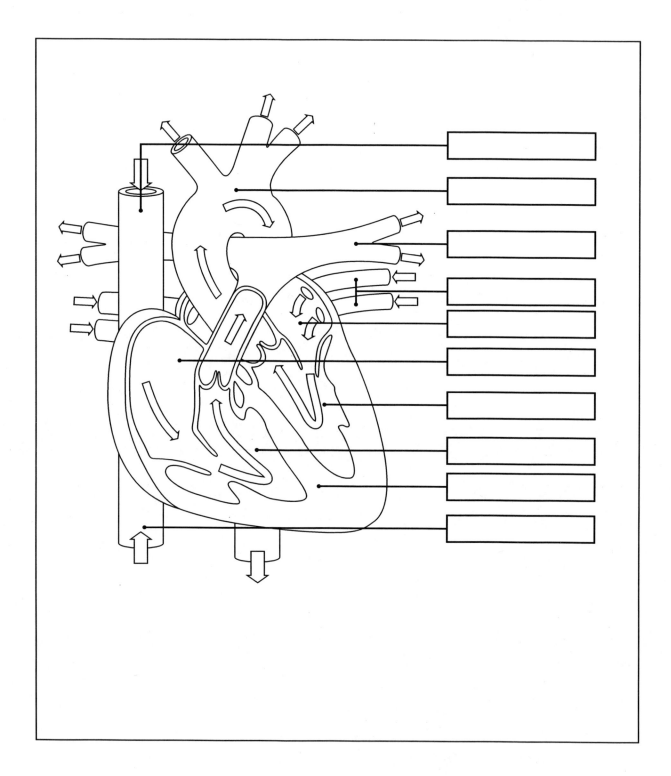

Chapter 9: The circulatory system   Pages 184–207

The heart is a pump that keeps blood circulating throughout the body. The arteries carry 'red' oxygenated blood out from the heart. The veins contain 'blue' deoxygenated blood returning to the heart. The artery and veins connecting the heart and lungs are the exceptions to the 'red/blue' blood rule.

1   Label the diagrams using the words listed below.

2   Colour the heart red and blue to show oxygenated and deoxygenated blood.

Stage 1

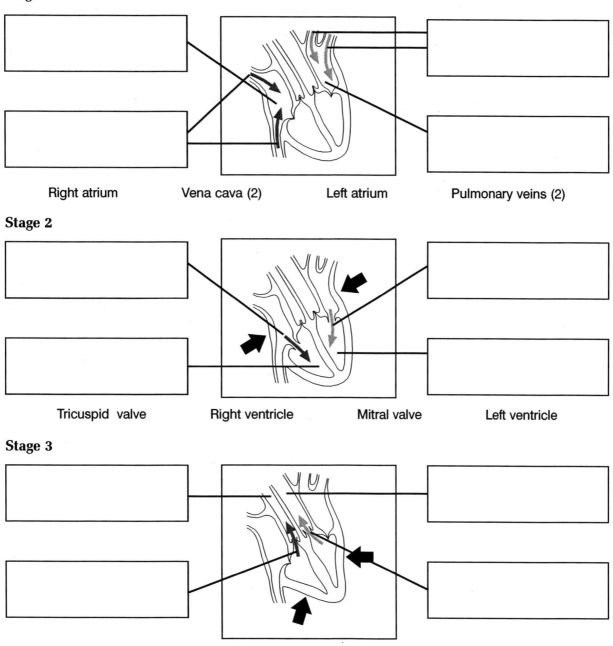

Right atrium   Vena cava (2)   Left atrium   Pulmonary veins (2)

Stage 2

Tricuspid valve   Right ventricle   Mitral valve   Left ventricle

Stage 3

Semilunar valves (right and left)   Pulmonary artery   Aorta

Chapter 9: The circulatory system   Pages 184–207

In order to supply our muscles with oxygen, blood is pumped through a network of blood vessels. Complete each sentence using the word arteries, capillaries or veins.

The walls of _ _ _ _ _ are non-elastic.

The walls of _ _ _ _ _ _ _ _ _ can contract to force blood forwards.

Blood is under high pressure in the _ _ _ _ _ _ _ _ _.

Oxygen passes through the thin walls of the _ _ _ _ _ _ _ _ _ _ _ into the tissues.

Some _ _ _ _ _ have valves to keep blood flowing in one direction.

Blood travels very slowly through the narrow _ _ _ _ _ _ _ _.

_ _ _ _ _ _ _ _ _ carry oxygenated blood from the heart.

How well does our heart pump?

Complete the following sentences and equation using these words as appropriate:

- cardiac output
- stroke volume
- heart rate.

The amount of blood pumped each beat is known as the _ _ _ _ _ _ _ _ _ _ _ _ _.

The number of times that the heart beats each minute is the _ _ _ _ _ _ _ _ _ _.

The amount of blood pumped to the body each minute is the _ _ _ _ _ _ _

_ _ _ _ _ _.

To work out the amount of blood going to our working muscles we use the following equation:

_ _ _ _ _ _ _ _ _ (ml per beat) x _ _ _ _ _ _ _ _ _ _ _ (beats per minute) = _ _ _ _ _ _ _ _ _ _ _ _ _ (litres per minute).

What is blood pressure?

Complete the following sentences.

Blood pressure is _____

When our blood pressure is high our heart has to _____

High blood pressure can be caused by:

- _____
- _____
- _____
- _____
- _____
- _____

Edexcel Sport Examined Teacher Support Pack © Beashel, Sibson and Taylor, Nelson Thornes Ltd, 2004

Blood has four components. Complete the table by giving a brief description of each and stating its main purpose.

Blood component	Description	Main purpose
Red cells		
White cells		
Plasma		
Platelets		

What does our blood do?

Our blood links all the tissues and organs of our body together. It has four main functions: transportation, protection, temperature regulation and maintaining the body's equilibrium.

Put these functions at the start of the correct section below and then fill in the missing words.

1 _ _ _ _ _ _ _ _ _ _ _ _ _ _ _

● carries _ _ _ _ _ _ _ _ _ _ _ _ from our digestive system to all our _ _ _ _ _

_ _ _ _ _ _.

● takes _ _ _ _ _ _ _ from our _ _ _ _ _ _ to our _ _ _ _ _ _ _ _ _ _ _ _ _ _ _ _ _.

● removes _ _ _ _ _ _ _ _ _ _ _ _ _ _ and _ _ _ _ _ _ products.

● takes _ _ _ _ _ _ _ _ _ _ to where they are needed.

2 _ _ _ _ _ _ _ _ _ _ _

● carries _ _ _ _ _ _ _ _ _ _ _ _ to sites of infection.

● carries _ _ _ _ _ _ _ _ _ _ _ _ to damaged areas to form _ _ _ _ _ _.

3 _

● carries _ _ _ _ _ away from _ _ _ _ _ _ _ _ _ _ _ _ _ _ _ _ and the body centre.

● maintains _ _ _ _ _ _ _ _ _ _ _ _ _ _ _ within the body.

4 Maintaining the body's _ _ _ _ _ _ _ _ _ _ _ _ _ _

● reduces the effect of _ _ _ _ _ _ _ _ _ _ _ _ _ in our _ _ _ _ _ _ _ _

_ _ _ _ _ _ _ _.

● regulates _ _ _ _ _ _ _ _ _ _ _ _ _ _ _ _.

Edexcel Sport Examined Teacher Support Pack © Beashel, Sibson and Taylor, Nelson Thornes Ltd, 2004

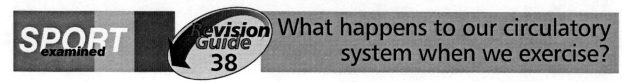

SPORT examined — Revision Guide 38 — What happens to our circulatory system when we exercise?

Chapter 9: The circulatory system   Pages 184–207

Fill in the missing words.

- The hormone _ _ _ _ _ _ _ _ _ _ _ _ is released even before we start to exercise. It prepares the body for action.

- _ _ _ _ _ _ _ _ _ _ _ increases – the heart beats more quickly.

- _ _ _ _ _ _ _ _ _ _ _ _ _ increases – the heart contracts more powerfully. It sends out a greater amount of blood with each contraction.

- _ _ _ _ _ _ _ _ _ _ _ _ _ _ _ _ _ _ increases – blood circulation speeds up and greater amounts of oxygen-carrying blood reach the working muscles.

- Blood flow to the _ _ _ _ _ _ _ _ _ _ system is reduced.

- Blood flow to the _ _ _ _ _ _ _ _ _ muscles is increased.

- _ _ _ _ _ _ _ _ _ _ _ _ _ to skin areas become enlarged, allowing excess heat from muscles and organs to be lost from the skin.

- During very hard exercise even these blood vessels will be reduced in size. Body _ _ _ _ _ _ _ _ _ _ _ _ _ will then rise very quickly. It can cause overheating and _ _ _ _ _ _ _ _ _.

- The oxygen going to the muscles can be up to _ times the resting amount.

- Blood flow can be increased up to _ _ times. Therefore, the working muscles can receive up to _ _ times the amount of oxygen they receive at rest.

Blood pressure and exercise

During sport the heart beats faster and pumps out more blood.
Blood pressure _ _ _ _ _ _ _ _ _ _. This is quite normal. However, regular sensible exercise linked with a healthy diet and lifestyle will actually lead to _ _ _ _ _ _ resting blood pressure.

Our blood circulation and exercise

As much as _ _ % of the heart's output may go to our working muscles during strenuous exercise. Training increases our body's ability to _ _ _ _ _ _ _ _ _ _ _ _ _ _ _ _ blood more efficiently.

Within the working muscles the _ _ _ _ _ _ _ reaches actual muscle fibres through the _ _ _ _ _ _ _ _ _ _ network. As a result of training this network increases, allowing more _ _ _ _ _ _ _ to be delivered to the working muscles.

Chapter 10: The respiratory system   Pages 208–219

Label and colour the diagram.

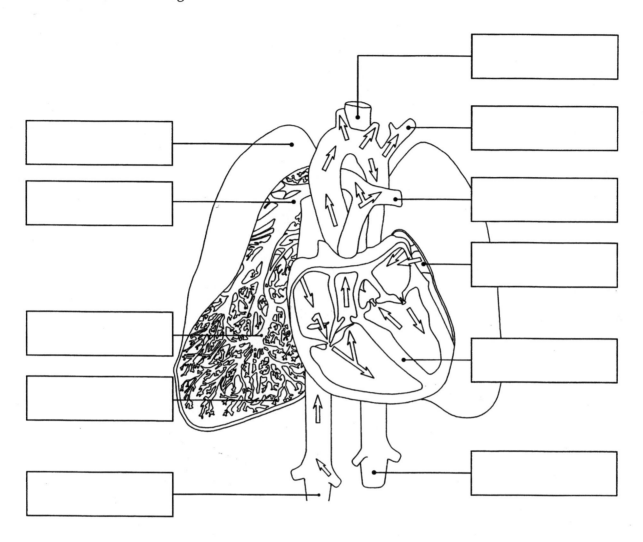

Edexcel Sport Examined Teacher Support Pack © Beashel, Sibson and Taylor, Nelson Thornes Ltd, 2004

Chapter 10: The respiratory system   Pages 208–219

Complete the following sentences.

Breathing is also called _ _ _ _ _ _ _ _ _ or _ _ _ _ _ _ _ _ _ _ _
_ _ _ _ _ _ _ _ _ _ _ _.

When breathing in (also called _ _ _ _ _ _ _ _ _ _ _ _):

• The _ _ _ _ _ _ _ _ _ _ _ _ muscles _ _ _ _ _ _ _ _ _, lifting the
  ribs _ _ _ _ _ _ _ _ and _ _ _ _ _ _ _ _ _. The chest _ _ _ _ _ _ _ _.

• The _ _ _ _ _ _ _ _ _ _ contracts. It pulls down and _ _ _ _ _ _ _ _ _ out.
  The chest _ _ _ _ _ _ _ _ some more.

• The lungs _ _ _ _ _ _ _ _ in size as the chest _ _ _ _ _ _ _.

• The pressure inside the lungs _ _ _ _ _ _ as they expand. Air is now _ _ _ _ _ _ _
  into the lungs through the _ _ _ _ and _ _ _ _ _.

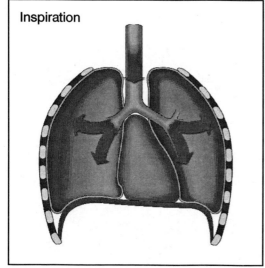

Inspiration

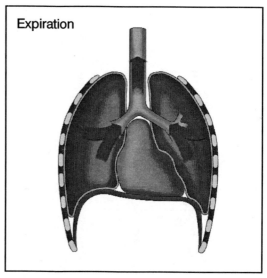

Expiration

When breathing out (also called _ _ _ _ _ _ _ _ _ _ _ _):

• The _ _ _ _ _ _ _ _ _ _ _ _ muscles _ _ _ _ _.The ribs move _ _ _ _ _ _ _ _ _ _ _
  and _ _ _ _ _ _ _ _. The chest gets _ _ _ _ _ _ _ _.

• The _ _ _ _ _ _ _ _ _ _ relaxes. It is pushed back into a _ _ _ _ _ _ position. The
  chest gets even _ _ _ _ _ _ _ _.

• The lungs _ _ _ _ _ _ _ _ _ in size as the chests gets _ _ _ _ _ _ _ _.

• The pressure inside the lungs _ _ _ _ _ _ _ _ _ _ _ as they get smaller. Air is
  forced _ _ _ of the lungs through the _ _ _ _ and _ _ _ _ _.

The composition of inhaled and exhaled air

The air we breathe in exchanges some of its oxygen for carbon dioxide in our lungs. The air we breathe out therefore contains less oxygen and more carbon dioxide. It also has much more water vapour, which is also a waste product from our cells.

Complete the table to show the relative composition of inhaled and exhaled air.

Inhaled air	%	Exhaled air	%
Nitrogen		Nitrogen	
Oxygen		Oxygen	
Carbon dioxide		Carbon dioxide	

What is tidal volume?

Fill in the missing words.

Tidal volume is the amount of _ _ _ _ _ _ _ _ _ _ _ _ _ _ _ _ _ _ in one _ _ _ _ _ _ _ _.
When we are resting, only _ _._ _ litres of air moves in and out of our lungs with each breath. Not
all of this reaches the _ _ _ _ _ _ _ _ _. Some remains in our _ _ _ _ _ and _ _ _ _ _ _ _ _.
If we start an activity, the body will need more _ _ _ _ _ _. We achieve this by breathing
more deeply which _ _ _ _ _ _ _ _ _ _ our tidal volume.

What is vital capacity?

Vital capacity is the _ _ _ _ _ _ _ _ _ _ _ _ _ _ _ _ of _ _ _ _ _ _ _ _ _ _ _ _ _ _
in or out of the _ _ _ _ _ _ in one _ _ _ _ _ _. It is our maximum tidal volume and is
usually about _ _._ _ litres in adults.

What is oxygen debt?

Oxygen debt is the amount of _ _ _ _ _ _ _ _ consumed during _ _ _ _ _ _ _ _ _
above what would _ _ _ _ _ _ _ _ _ _ _ have been _ _ _ _ _ _ _ _ _ during the
same _ _ _ _ _ _ _ at _ _ _ _ _.

Taking in _ _ _ _ _ _ allows us to remove the _ _ _ _ _ _ _ _ _ _ _ _, replace the
oxygen _ _ _ _ _ _ _ _ _ _ in our bodies and to build up other muscle supplies.

Edexcel Sport Examined Teacher Support Pack © Beashel, Sibson and Taylor, Nelson Thornes Ltd, 2004

Supplying oxygen to the working muscles

Chapter 10: The respiratory system   Pages 208–219

Complete the following sentences.

We breathe in and out about __ __ times a minute at rest.

When exercising very hard, breathing rate can increase to __ __ times a minute.

The amount of air breathed in can increase from __ litres to __ __ __ litres a minute.

Training can improve breathing.

The two stages of oxygen supply

The respiratory system needs two stages to supply oxygen to the working muscles and all the other body cells.

Stage 1 is called _ _ _ _ _ _ _ _ _ or _ _ _ _ _ _ _ _ _ _ respiration.

We know it as _ _ _ _ _ _ _ _ _ _. It includes:

- getting _ _ _ _ _ _ into and out of the lungs
- exchanging _ _ _ _ _ _ _ and _ _ _ _ _ _ _ _ _ _ _ _ _ _ _ in the lungs
- getting oxygen into the _ _ _ _ _ _ _ _ _ _ _ _.

Stage 2 is called _ _ _ _ _ _ _ _ _ or _ _ _ _ _ respiration. It includes:

- getting oxygen into the _ _ _ _ _ _ _ _ _
- exchanging _ _ _ _ _ _ _ and _ _ _ _ _ _ _ _ _ _ _ _ _ _ _ in the cells
- removing _ _ _ _ _ _ _ _ _ _ _ _ _ _ _ and waste.

Internal (or cell) respiration

In this process we use oxygen to release the energy from glucose inside our body cells. This can be shown as:

_ _ _ _ _ _ _ _ + Oxygen = _ _ _ _ _ _ _ + Carbon dioxide + _ _ _ _ _ _

Edexcel Sport Examined Teacher Support Pack © Beashel, Sibson and Taylor, Nelson Thornes Ltd, 2004

Chapter 10: The respiratory system   Pages 208–219

Our bodies need energy so that our muscles can contract and make our body work. We can provide this energy by using either one of our two energy systems: the anaerobic or the aerobic system.

Complete the following definitions.

When we use the anaerobic system, _____

_____ .

When we use the aerobic system, _____

_____ .

The two energy systems and sport

The energy we need for different sports varies a great deal.

Complete the table below to show the energy system used for each activity. Then choose two more activities of your own and add the correct energy system for them.

Sporting activity	Energy system used
Shot putt	
100-metre sprint swim	
Marathon run	
Hockey	

Our anaerobic system works without oxygen and supplies our muscles with energy quickly. In contrast, our aerobic system must have oxygen in order to work and only supplies energy slowly to our muscles.

Oxygen debt and lactic acid

We can continue to perform strenuous activity for some time even when we run out

of _ _ _ _ _ _ by using the store of _ _ _ _ _ _ _ _ _ in the body.

But the disadvantage is that we also produce _ _ _ _ _ _ _ _ _ _ _ _. This makes

our _ _ _ _ _ _ _ _ _ _ _ _ and eventually we have to _ _ _ _ the activity.

In the recovery period after exercise we take in extra _ _ _ _ _ _ _ which is used

to _ _ _ _ _ _ _ the painful _ _ _ _ _ _ _ _ _ _ into simple _ _ _ _ _

_ _ _ _ _ _ _ _. The oxygen required to do this is called our _ _ _ _ _ _ _

_ _ _ _ _.

Edexcel Sport Examined Teacher Support Pack © Beashel, Sibson and Taylor, Nelson Thornes Ltd, 2004

Chapter 11: Bones   Pages 220–235

Complete the sentences using the words listed below.

- ossification
- bone
- collagen
- calcium
- cartilage.

In the embryo most of the skeleton is made of _ _ _ _ _ _ _ _ _ _. As the baby grows into childhood and adulthood, this changes to _ _ _ _. This process is known as _ _ _ _ _ _ _ _ _ _ _ _ _. Mature bone contains _ _ _ _ _ _ _ to give hardness and _ _ _ _ _ _ _ _ fibres to make it strong and light.

The composition of a long bone

Label the diagram, matching the correct terms with the descriptions provided.

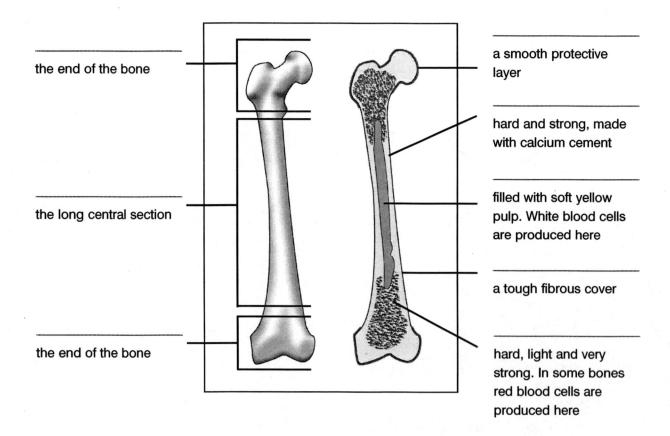

the end of the bone

the long central section

the end of the bone

a smooth protective layer

hard and strong, made with calcium cement

filled with soft yellow pulp. White blood cells are produced here

a tough fibrous cover

hard, light and very strong. In some bones red blood cells are produced here

Complete the sentences in each section.

Our bones and age

Our bones change even when we are fully grown. They _ _ _ _ _ to any pressure that
is put upon them by _ _ _ _ _ _ _ _ _ _ _ _ _ _ _ _ and becoming stronger.
Regular _ _ _ _ _ _ _ _-_ _ _ _ _ _ _ _ _ exercise throughout life will keep our bones
strong and healthy. If we do not strengthen our bones enough when we are young they may
weaken and break easily when we are older.

Our bones and gender

Overall men have _ _ _ _ _ _ _ _ _ _ _ _ _ _ _ _ _ _ and are _ _ _ _ _ _ _ _
than women. Men also have _ _ _ _ _ _ _ bones than women. At puberty
the _ _ _ _ _ _ _ _ _ _ _ _ _ in girls becomes wider to make childbearing easier.
This changes the angle of the _ _ _ _ _ _ _ _ _ and makes the running action less
_ _ _ _ _ _ _ _ _ _.

Our bones and diet

Protein in our diet is important for the _ _ _ _ _ _ _, _ _ _ _ _ _ _ and
_ _ _ _ _ _ _ _ _ _ _ _ _ _ _ _ _ _ of all our tissues, including bones.

Our bones need a regular supply of _ _ _ _ _ _ _ in the diet. Lack of _ _ _ _ _ _ _ _ _
will result in bone _ _ _ _ _ _ _ _. We also need vitamin _ which helps the bones
absorb the _ _ _ _ _ _ _ _.

Our bones, body shape and body weight

The size of our skeleton is largely decided by _ _ _ _ _ _ _ _ _ _. If we follow
a _ _ _ _ _ _ _ _ _ diet we are likely to reach our maximum _ _ _ _ _ _ _ and
maximum bone _ _ _ _ _.

Our bones and exercise

_ _ _ _ _ _ _ _ _ _ helps increase bone _ _ _ _ _ _ and bone _ _ _ _ _ _ _ _ and
therefore bone _ _ _ _ _ _ _ _ _ _. It has no effect on bone _ _ _ _ _ _ _ _.
Lifting _ _ _ _ _ _ _ _ _ _ _ _ _ _ _, taking part in _ _ _ _ _ _ _ _ _ _ _
_ _ _ _ _ _ _ _ sports and long-distance _ _ _ _ _ _ _ _ _ _ _ _ _ _ can all damage
the _ _ _ _ _ _ _ _ plates in the bones and lead to _ _ _ _ _ _ _ _ _ _ growth.

If we are unable to exercise through injury or illness we will lose both bone _ _ _ _ _ and
_ _ _ _ _ _ _ _ _.

Our bones and sport

Our body is made up of very many bones of different shapes and sizes.
The _ _ _ _ _ _ _ _ _ _ _ _ of bones enable us to perform the very _ _ _ _ _ _
movements necessary for darts as well as making a full-blooded tackle in rugby.
The _ _ _ _ _ _ _ the bone, the greater the range of movement possible and the greater
the amount of _ _ _ _ _ _ produced.

Edexcel Sport Examined Teacher Support Pack © Beashel, Sibson and Taylor, Nelson Thornes Ltd, 2004

Chapter 11: Bones   Pages 220–235

1 Label the skeleton.
2 Choose four colours and shade each type of bone in a different colour.

Key

Long bone ☐   Short bone ☐   Irregular bone ☐   Flat (plate) bone ☐

Edexcel Sport Examined Teacher Support Pack © Beashel, Sibson and Taylor, Nelson Thornes Ltd, 2004

There are four different types of bone. Draw an example of each in the boxes below.

List the examples from the skeleton and briefly describe what they do (you should relate this to sport if possible).

	Type of bone _____ **Examples** _____ _____ **What they do** _____ _____
	Type of bone _____ **Examples** _____ _____ **What they do** _____ _____
	Type of bone _____ **Examples** _____ _____ **What they do** _____ _____
	Type of bone _____ **Examples** _____ _____ **What they do** _____ _____

113

The vertebral column

Complete the sentences using the words listed below:

disc   33   spinal   shock absorber   vertebrae

Our vertebral or _____ column is made up of ___ bones called _____.

Between each bone is a thick circle of tough cartilage called a _____. It acts as a _____

_____.

What does the vertebral column do?

List the five functions of our vertebral column.

The vertebral column:

1 _____

2 _____

3 _____

4 _____

5 _____

Label each section of the vertebral column and shade each section in a different colour.

The vertebral column is important to all sporting movements. It has many joints and is both flexible and strong. This allows us to bend and stretch our bodies into very many different positions.

Give an example from sport of the vertebral column providing

● strength

_____

_____

_____

● flexibilty.

_____

_____

_____

Edexcel Sport Examined Teacher Support Pack © Beashel, Sibson and Taylor, Nelson Thornes Ltd, 2004

The five functions of our skeleton are

- shape
- protection
- movement
- support
- blood production.

Put these functions at the start of the correct section below and then fill in the missing words. Write a sentence to describe the importance of each for sport.

1 _ _ _ _ _

- Our body needs a _ _ _ _ _ _ _ _ _ _.
- The skeleton gives _ _ _ _ _ to our _ _ _ _ _ _.
- The bones enable us to achieve a _ _ _ _ _ _ _ _ _ _ _ _.

Importance for sport _____

2 _ _ _ _ _ _ _ _ _ _ _

- Delicate _ _ _ _ _ _ _ need protection.
- Our cranium protects the _ _ _ _ _ _.
- Our _ _ _ _ _ _ _ _ _ _ _ _ _ _ _ _ protects our spinal cord.
- Our _ _ _ _ _ _ _ _ protects our _ _ _ _ _ and _ _ _ _ _ _.

Importance for sport _____

3 _ _ _ _ _ _ _ _ _

- Our _ _ _ _ _ _ _ _ _ use our bones to cause _ _ _ _ _ _ _ _ _ _.
- Our muscles are _ _ _ _ _ _ _ _ _ _ to the skeleton.
- The skeleton is _ _ _ _ _ _ _ _ which allows a wide range of movement.
- Different _ _ _ _ _ _ allow different types of _ _ _ _ _ _ _ _ _.

Importance for sport _____

4 _ _ _ _ _ _ _

- The skeleton holds our _ _ _ _ _ _ _ _ _ _ _ _ in place.
- The _ is central in supporting much of our body.

Importance for sport _____

5 _ _ _ _ _ _ _ _ _ _ _ _ _ _ _ _

Red and white _ _ _ _ _ _ _ _ _ _ _ _ are produced in the _ _ _ _ _ _ _ _ _ _ _ _ of the _ _ _ _ _, _ _ _ _ _ _ _ _ _ _ _ and _ _ _ _ _ _.

Importance for sport _____

Edexcel Sport Examined Teacher Support Pack © Beashel, Sibson and Taylor, Nelson Thornes Ltd, 2004

A joint is _____ .

The function of joints is _____ .

There are three types of joint. These are:

Type of joint	Example
1	
2	
3	

How do our synovial joints work?

Look at the diagrams below.

Colour each diagram using a different colour for each part.

The hip joint   **The knee joint**

Synovial membrane   Synovial fliud

Ligaments

Joint capsule

Hyaline cartilage

1 Look at each of the types of synovial joint shown below.

2 Name each type of joint.

3 Give an example.

4 Describe how each is used in sport.

The first example has been partly completed for you.

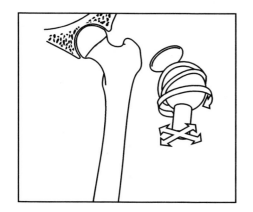

Name   Hinge joint

Example   Elbow

How it is used in sport

Name

Example

How it is used in sport

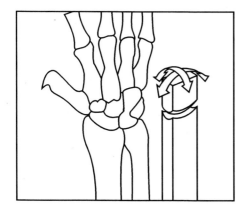

Name

Example

How it is used in sport

Edexcel Sport Examined Teacher Support Pack © Beashel, Sibson and Taylor, Nelson Thornes Ltd, 2004

What are the different types of cartilage found in the body?

Cartilage is a tough but flexible tissue found on the ends of bones and as a pad between bones.

Hyaline cartilage is _____

_____

_____

Cartilage pads in the _ _ _ _ _ _ _ _ _ _ _ _ _ _ _ _ _ _ and _ _ _ _ _ act as

_ _ _ _ _ _ _ _ _ _ _ _ _ _ _ _ _.

Describe the importance of each type of cartilage in sport.

_____

_____

_____

Ligaments and tendons

Ligaments are bands of _ _ _ _ _ _ _ _ _ _ _ _ _ _ _ _ _ _ _ _ _ _ _ which bind our

_ _ _ _ _ _ together at _ _ _ _ _ _ _ _. Some ligaments form a _ _ _ _ _ _ _ _ which

surrounds the joint and contains _ _ _ _ _ _ _ _ _ _ _ _ _ _ _ _. Other ligaments

remain separate outside the _ _ _ _ _ _ _ but also hold the joint _ _ _ _ _ _ _.

The ligaments make joints more _ _ _ _ _ _ _ by preventing _ _ _ _ _ _ _ _ _ _ _

movement. They also attempt to direct movement. In general, the more ligaments around a

joint the _ _ _ _ _ _ _ _ the joint will be.

Describe the importance of ligaments in sport. Explain the cause and effect of ligament injury.

_____

_____

Tendons are strong _ _ _ _ _ _ of _ _ _ _ _ _ _ _ _ _ _ _ _ _ _ _ _ _. They allow us to

apply the _ _ _ _ _ _ of the contracting _ _ _ _ _ _ _ to the bones at the _ _ _ _ _ _.

Describe the importance of tendons in sport.

_____

_____

Explain the cause and effect of tendon injury.

_____

_____

Edexcel Sport Examined Teacher Support Pack © Beashel, Sibson and Taylor, Nelson Thornes Ltd, 2004

Label the diagrams to show the types of movement in each sporting situation

Complete the table by:

1 naming the muscle type which matches each description

2 saying where the muscle type is found

3 giving an example of the importance of each in sport.

Description	Muscle type	Where this muscle type is found	Importance in sport
Muscle fibres never get tired (fatigue)			
Muscle fibres under our control. Used to perform movement in sport			
Muscle fibres operate automatically			

Muscle fibres

Insert the words fast twitch or slow twitch to complete each sentence.

_ _ _ _ _   _ _ _ _ _ _ _ fibres contract very quickly.

_ _ _ _ _   _ _ _ _ _ _ _ fibres are capable of repeated contractions over a long period of time.

_ _ _ _ _   _ _ _ _ _ _ _ fibres are capable of stronger and more powerful muscle contractions.

_ _ _ _ _   _ _ _ _ _ _ _ fibres fatigue rapidly.

The oxygen supply to _ _ _ _ _   _ _ _ _ _ _ _ fibres is very good.

A marathon runner will have a greater proportion of _ _ _ _ _   _ _ _ _ _ _ _ fibres in his/her leg muscles.

A sprinter will have a greater proportion of _ _ _ _ _   _ _ _ _ _ _ _ fibres in his/her leg muscles.

Edexcel Sport Examined Teacher Support Pack © Beashel, Sibson and Taylor, Nelson Thornes Ltd, 2004

Chapter 13: Muscles and muscle action   Pages 250–267

The diagrams below show the main muscle groups in the body.

1 Label the diagrams with the names of the muscles.

2 Shade each muscle a different colour.

3 Give an example of an action each muscle might perform in sport.

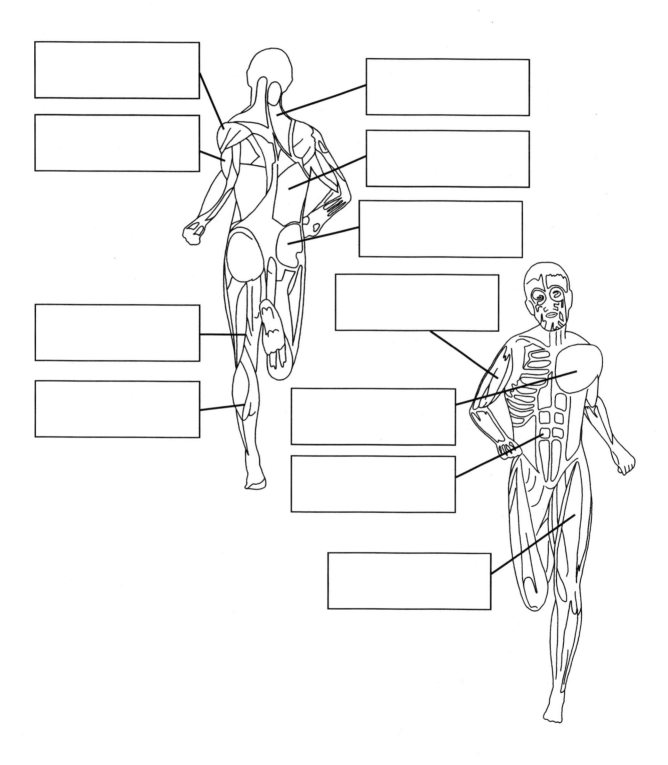

SPORT examined · Revision Guide 56 · How do our muscles work together?

Chapter 13: Muscles and muscle action   Pages 250–267

Prime movers and antagonists

Our muscles can pull by contracting, but they cannot push. Our muscles take a different role depending on the movement we are performing.

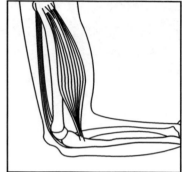

Look at the diagram and fill in the missing words.

In this isotonic action, the biceps muscle is the __ __ __ __ __ __ __ __ __ __ __. This muscle contracts to start the movement. The triceps muscle is the __ __ __ __ __ __ __ __ __ __ __ __ __. This muscle __ __ __ __ __ __ __ to allow the movement to take place.

Complete this description.

At take-off a high jumper extends her leg at the knee. During this movement the quadriceps is the __ __ __ __ __   __ __ __ __ __ __ and the hamstring is the __ __ __ __ __ __ __ __ __ __ __.

Antagonistic pairs and sport

Although we say that the antagonist muscle relaxes to allow the prime mover to work, we know that it actually keeps some fibres contracting.

1 Explain why this happens.

_____

_____

2 Give an example of what can go wrong if the system fails.

_____

_____

How are our muscles attached to our bones?

Muscles are attached to bones by tendons.

The origin is at one end of the muscle. The insertion is at the other end.

How can we tell which end is which?

The origin is the end which

_____

The insertion is the end which

_____

Edexcel Sport Examined Teacher Support Pack © Beashel, Sibson and Taylor, Nelson Thornes Ltd, 2004

Posture and muscle tone

Chapter 13: Muscles and muscle action   Pages 250–267

Muscle tone is important for good posture.

Muscle tone is produced when _____

_____

Read the description of muscle tone on page 260 of *Edexcel Sport Examined* and explain it in your own words.

_____

_____

_____

_____

Posture

Complete the sentences to explain the importance of good posture.

If we have good posture we can keep our bodies _ _ _ _ _ _ _ easily by keeping our
_ _ _ _ _ _ _ _ _ _ _ _ _ _ _ _ _ _ over our base of support. Good posture reduces
the strain on our _ _ _ _ _ _ _ _ _, _ _ _ _ _ _ _ _ _ and _ _ _ _ _ _ _ _ _ _. It
allows our body systems to work more easily and makes us less tired. Good _ _ _ _ _ _ _
_ _ _ _ _, particularly in the lower back, leg and abdominal muscles, will help posture.

We feel better about ourselves when we have good posture as it plays an important role in creating
a _ and _ _ _ _ _-_ _ _ _ _. When we
slouch, the upper back muscle must _ _ _ _ _ _ _ _ _ to move the _ _ _ _ _ to the
_ _ _ _ _ _ _ _ posture. If we continue to slouch, the muscles will gradually _ _ _ _ _
to that position. Poor posture may then become _ _ _ _ _ _ _ _ _ _.

Posture and sport

Posture is important in two ways. Explain each.

Starting position

_____

_____

Position during the activity

_____

_____

123

Edexcel Sport Examined Teacher Support Pack © Beashel, Sibson and Taylor, Nelson Thornes Ltd, 2004

Everyday exercise

Our voluntary muscles can _ _ _ _ _ in order to cope with activity.

When we put our muscles under an increased _ _ _ _ _ _ they _ _ _ _ _ _ to the new _ _ _ _ _ _ _ _ .

The effect of training

If we train and exercise regularly

_____

_____

If we stop exercising

_____

_____

Our _ _ _ _ _ _ _ _ _ _ muscles become _ _ _ _ _ _ _ _ _ the more they
are _ _ _ _ _ _ _ _ _ _ . If we train regularly over a long period we
will _ _ _ _ _ _ _ our muscles.

Our muscles increase in _ _ _ _ , _ _ _ _ _ _ _ _ _ _ and _ _ _ _ _ _ _ _ _ _
when we follow a regular strength training programme. This is called
muscle _ _ _ _ _ _ _ _ _ _ _ _ .

What happens to our muscular system as we exercise?

Make a list below.

- _____
- _____
- _____
- _____
- _____
- _____
- _____
- _____
- _____
- _____

Edexcel Sport Examined Teacher Support Pack © Beashel, Sibson and Taylor, Nelson Thornes Ltd, 2004

1 **(a)** A state of complete mental, physical and social well-being, and not merely the absence of disease or infirmity

   (b) A form of physical activity done primarily to improve one's health and physical fitness

   (c) The ability to meet the demands of the environment

   (d) How well a task is completed

   (e) The ability to exercise the entire body for long periods of time

   (f) Amount of force that can be applied by a muscle group to overcome resistance

   (g) The range of movement possible at a joint

   (h) Ability to use voluntary muscles many times without getting tired

   (i) The percentage of body weight which is fat, muscle and bone

   (j) Sensible diet, increase exercise.

   Maximum score: 11

2 **(a)** The ability to change the position of the body quickly and to control the movement of the whole body

   (b) 'The ability to retain the centre of mass (gravity) of the body above the base of support with reference to static (stationary) or dynamic (changing) conditions of movement, shape and orientation.' (Edexcel.) A simpler definition is the ability to retain equilibrium, whether stationary or moving.

   (c) The ability to use two or more body parts together

   (d) The level of fitness necessary for good health

   (e) The ability to do strength performances quickly. Power = Strength × Speed.

   (f) The time between the presentation of a stimulus and the onset of a movement

   (g) The level of fitness necessary for success in a specific sport

   (h) 'The differential rate at which an individual is able to perform a movement or cover a distance in a period of time'. (Edexcel.) More simply, speed is the ability to move all or part of the body as quickly as possible.

   (i) Power, flexibility

   (j) Reaction time, co-ordination, speed.

   Maximum score: 10

3 **(a)** Multistage (Beep), Harvard Step, Cooper 12-minute Run

   (b) Handgrip Dynamometer, Repetition Max

   (c) Standing Broad Jump, Standing Vertical Jump

   (d) Press-up, NCF Abdominal Curl

   (e) Sit and Reach, Shoulder Hyperextension

   (f) 50m Sprint

   (g) Illinois Agility Run

   (h) Alternate Hand Wall Toss

   (i) Computer; Ruler Drop Test

   (j) Stork Stand.

   Maximum score: 10

Edexcel Sport Examined Teacher Support Pack © Beashel, Sibson and Taylor, Nelson Thornes Ltd, 2004

4 (a) Specificity, Progression, Overload, Reversibility, Tedium

   (b) Frequency, Intensity, Time, Type

   (c) Warm-up, skill development, fitness, warm-down

   (d) Training programmes must be designed to develop the specific fitness, strength and skills required for our sport and must also meet our own particular needs

   (e) The level of training that we need to work at to suit our individual needs

   (f) 220 minus age (boys), 226 minus age (girls)

   (g) Maximum Heart Rate

   (h) 60%

   (i) 80%

   (j) Aerobic.

Maximum score: 20

5 (a) Continuous; *marathon running

   (b) Fartlek/ speedplay; *games (football, hockey, etc.)

   (c) Interval; *800m

   (d) Circuit; *all games

   (e) Weight training; *sprinting, rugby, etc.

   (f) Plyometrics; *volleyball, high jump

   (g) Isotonic

   (h) Warm-up, main activity, cool-down

   (i) Length of time for cardiorespiratory system to return to normal after activity

   (j) (i)   Lactic acid
        (ii) Muscle fatigue (pain, stiffness).

*Maximum score: 13 (*19)*

6 (a) Carbohydrates; *pasta

   (b) Fats; *cheese

   (c) Protein; *meat

   (d) Vitamins

   (e) Minerals

   (f) Fibre

   (g) Water

   (h) They would lose weight

   (i) Eat less; exercise more

   (j) Carbohydrate loading.

Maximum score: 11

7 (a) Cigarette smoking (nicotine)

   (b) Alcohol

   (c) Alcohol

Edexcel Sport Examined Teacher Support Pack © Beashel, Sibson and Taylor, Nelson Thornes Ltd, 2004

(d) Diuretics

(e) Anabolic steroids

(f) Amphetamines/stimulants

(g) Analgesics

(h) Blood doping

(i) Beta blockers

(j) Marijuana.

Maximum score: 10

8 **(a)** Rest, Ice, Compression, Elevation

(b) Danger, Response, Airway, Breathing, Circulation

(c) Open, closed

(d) Dislocation, sprain

(e) Concussion

(f) Strain/tear

(g) Dehydration/heat exhaustion

(h) Recovery position

(i) Blisters

(j) Tennis elbow.

Maximum score: 19

9 **(a)** Takes oxygen and nutrients to every cell; removes carbon dioxide and other waste from the cells; carries hormones; maintains temperature and fluid levels, fights infection.

(b) De/oxygenated blood; veins have valves; arteries have thicker walls; veins go to the heart, arteries away from the heart (note exceptions to/from lungs).

(c) Pumps blood

(d) Atrium

(e) Ventricle

(f) Left

(g) Pulmonary artery

(h) Pulmonary vein

(i) Semilunar; tricuspid

(j) Ventricles.

Maximum score: 17

10 **(a)** Transportation; temperature regulation; acidic balance

(b) Plasma

(c) Hæmoglobin

(d) Red blood cells

(e) White blood cells

(f) Platelets

(g) The pressure created when the heart pumps blood through the arteries – the pressure of blood flow through the arteries

(h) It tells us how hard the heart is having to work and indicates the health of our arteries, veins and capillaries

Edexcel Sport Examined Teacher Support Pack © Beashel, Sibson and Taylor, Nelson Thornes Ltd, 2004

(i) Age; exercise; stress and tension; cigarette smoking; diet

(j) Hypertension.

Maximum score: 16

11 (a) Trachea

(b) Alveoli

(c) Contracts

(d) Lift upwards and outwards

(e) Lower

(f) Carbon dioxide

(g) Tidal volume

(h) Vital capacity

(i) Cell respiration

(j) Lactic acid.

Maximum score: 10

12 (a) Protects; gives shape; supports; permits movement; blood cell production

(b) Ossification

(c) Periosteum

(d) Short

(e) Long

(f) Flat

(g) Irregular

(h) Provides calcium which strengthens bone

(i) Cartilage

(j) Shoulder girdle.

Maximum score: 15

13 (a) Femur

(b) Phalanges

(c) Humerus

(d) Metacarpals

(e) Radius/ulna

(f) Sternum

(g) Tibia and fibula

(h) Clavicle

(i) Scapula

(j) Patella.

Maximum score: 12

14 (a) Shoulder or hip

(b) Hinge

(c) Humerus and scapula

(d) Between the atlas and axis bones

(e) Join muscles to bone

(f) Join bone to bone

(g) Adduction

(h) Extension

(i) Flexion

(j) Rotation.

Maximum score: 11

15 (a) Voluntary, involuntary, cardiac

(b) Biceps/triceps, quadriceps/hamstrings

(c) Fast twitch, slow twitch

(d) Slow twitch

(e) Continuous slight contraction of our muscles

(f) Choose two from: enhance body shape; develop self-esteem; improve sporting performance.

(g) Basketball, sprinting

(h) Marathon running

(i) Biceps

(j) Quadriceps.

Maximum score: 15

16 (a) Quadriceps

(b) Gluteals

(c) Deltoid

(d) Latissimus dorsi

(e) Trapezius

(f) Pectorals

(g) Hamstrings

(h) Biceps

(i) Triceps

(j) Abdominals.

Maximum score: 10

Edexcel Sport Examined Teacher Support Pack © Beashel, Sibson and Taylor, Nelson Thornes Ltd, 2004

2 Reasons for taking part in sport and physical activity

| 1 | D | **2** | B | 3 | B | **4** | A | | *4 marks* |

5   **(a)** *Competition*: able to test himself against others,
e.g. in inter-school matches.   *2 marks*

Physical challenge: competing against own best performance,
e.g. higher scores on floor or high bar.   *2 marks*

Aesthetic enjoyment: the pleasure gained from movement,
e.g. completing a routine in good style.   *2 marks*

(b) Any two from:

- develops physical qualities to cope with everyday life

- weight control

- improves body shape

- feel and look good

- stress reduction.   *2 marks*

(c) Any two from: co-operation, competition, physical challenge,
aesthetic appreciation, friendships and social mixing.   *2 marks*

Total 14 marks

6   **(a)** *Co-operation*: working with others, e.g. teamwork in distance race
or helping organise the younger girls.   *2 marks*

Competition: testing her ability against others, e.g. in races and
competitions of different sorts.   *2 marks*

Friendship: contact with others, e.g. sharing similar experiences at events.   *2 marks*

(b) Any four from: feel good, enhanced body shape, muscle tone, weight control,
minimum levels of strength, stamina, flexibility.   *4 marks*

(c) Quality of movement in running: smooth, effortless, rhythmic,
pleasurable to the eye.   *2 marks*

(d) *Stress*: unhealthy pressure caused by factors such as family,
work or finance.   *2 marks*

Reduction of blood pressure, relaxation, tension reduction,
fresh look at worries.   *2 marks*

(e) Testing own ability – mental and physical   *2 marks*

Running in order to achieve a better time or to win a race.   *2 marks*

Total 20 marks

3 Health, fitness, exercise and performance

| 1 | C | **2** | A | 3 | D | **4** | A | | *4 marks* |

5   **(a)** The level of fitness necessary for good health.   *1 mark*

(b) Any one from: tennis improves cardiovascular fitness, muscular strength,
muscular endurance, flexibility, body composition.   *1 mark*

Edexcel Sport Examined Teacher Support Pack © Beashel, Sibson and Taylor, Nelson Thornes Ltd, 2004

(c) Any four from:

- *Cardiovascular fitness*: practising or playing over a long period of time develops stamina.

- *Muscular strength*: strength is developed by hitting the ball hard.

- *Muscular endurance*: practising or playing for a period of time develops endurance in racket arm and upper body generally.

- *Flexibility*: many instances of stretching for ball, e.g. to play shot or to serve

- *Body composition*: exercise uses calories; reduces fat; builds muscle; enhances body shape. *8 marks*

Total 14 marks

6 (a) *Health*: a state of complete mental, physical and social well being, and not merely the absence of disease or infirmity. *1 mark*

(b) Any three from: sensible diet, regular exercise, rest and sleep, limit alcohol, no smoking or social drugs, improve stress management. *3 marks*

(c) *Exercise*: a form of physical activity done primarily to improve one's health and physical fitness. *1 mark*

(d) Any two from each category, such as:

- *Physical*: stronger heart, more efficient breathing, stronger muscles, better flexibility

- *Mental*: stress relief, enjoyable challenge, range of emotional experience

- *Social*: meet others, develop friendships, co-operation. *6 marks*

7 (a) *Cardiovascular fitness*: improved by whole-body exercise, e.g. running, swimming, cycling.

(b) *Muscular endurance*: improved by training with light weights and a high number of repetitions.

(c) *Flexibility*: improved by stretching muscles beyond normal range of movement.

3 marks

(d)

Component of health-related fitness	Importance to high jump
Cardiovascular fitness	not important in event except to complete training
Muscular endurance:	power at take-off is dependent on strength and speed
Flexibility	Important at take-off to exert force over full range and in moving over bar
Body composition	light body weight, minimum fat, maximum strength from muscle

6 marks

Total 20 marks

Edexcel Sport Examined Teacher Support Pack © Beashel, Sibson and Taylor, Nelson Thornes Ltd, 2004

4 Skill-related fitness

1 C   **2** B   **3** D   **4** C   *4 marks*

5 **(a)** **i** Sprinters need a short reaction time to get a good start.   *1 mark*

ii Power: jumper needs an explosive burst of energy to raise centre of gravity.   *1 mark*

iii Balance: surfer needs good dynamic balance to remain on the board.   *1 mark*

(b)

Component of fitness	Health- or skill-related	Use of component by basketball player
Cardiovascular fitness	Health	
	SR	Able to drive for the basket with strength and speed
	SR	Able to perform complex movements with the ball
Agility		

7 marks

Total 14 marks

6 **(a)** **i** *Speed*: ability to move quickly around the pitch.

ii *Reaction time*: ability to respond to position of players and ball.

iii *Co-ordination*: ability to control, pass or move the ball easily.

iv *Power*: the ability to accelerate, jump or kick the ball hard.   *4 marks*

(b) **i** *Power*: Standing Broad Jump or Vertical Jump

ii *Agility*: Illinois Agility Run

iii *Balance*: Stork Stand

iv *Speed*: 50-metre Speed Test.   *4 marks*

(c) **i** *Power*: weights at speed or plyometrics.

ii *Speed*: weights at speed or plyometrics.

iii *Agility*: practising the skills at speed.

iv *Balance*: practising the skills of the game.   *4 marks*

(d) Any four from:

– *Muscular strength*: the amount of force a muscle can exert against a resistance. Used when kicking, tackling or heading the ball

– *Muscular endurance*: the ability to use voluntary muscles many times without getting tired. Used when repeating skills through the duration of the game

– *Flexibility*: the range of movement possible at a joint. Used in all skilful movements with body at full stretch

– *Cardiovascular endurance*: the ability to exercise the entire body for long periods of time. Used to maintain skill levels throughout the game

– *Body composition*: the percentage of body weight which is fat, muscle and bone. Having the appropriate body build for the position on the field.   *8 marks*

Total 20 marks

132

5 Principles of training

1 C   **2** D   **3** B   **4** A   *4 marks*

5 **(a)** Any three from the following:

- *Specificity*: training for our own particular sport – e.g. dribbling relay
- *Progression*: increase training gradually – e.g. increasing weights lifted
- *Overload*: work harder than normal – e.g. interval sprint training
- *Reversibility*: we lose fitness if we stop training. – e.g. maintain fitness programme
- *Tedium*: make training interesting – e.g. play volleyball.   *6 marks*

     (b) Aerobic threshold: 122; anaerobic threshold: 163.   *2 marks*

     (c) *Periodisation*: dividing up an annual training programme into parts, e.g. pre-season, peak season and off-season.   *2 marks*

                                                 Total 14 marks

6 **(a)** *Frequency*: any two from: train at least three times a week, allow time for recovery, avoid training on consecutive days   *2 marks*

          Intensity: any two from: work harder than normal, start from current fitness, understand target zones   *2 marks*

          Time: any two from: increase length of training session, a minimum of 20 minutes, ensure heart working heart rate is raised significantly   *2 marks*

          Type: any two from: relevant fitness training, appropriate skills practices, modified games.   *2 marks*

     (b) *Warm-up*: e.g. light jogging, flexibility exercises.
Fitness training: e.g. shuttle runs, circuit training.
Skill development: e.g. passing in pairs, heading under pressure
Game: e.g. modified game, one touch, 4 v 4
Warm-down: e.g. light jogging, flexibility exercises.   *10 marks*

     (c) *Pre-season*: any two from: focus on fitness, concentrate on muscular endurance, power and speed, develop techniques, skills and strategies.

          Peak season: any two from: emphasise speed, practise skills at speed and in competitive situations, extra fitness sessions if insufficient matches.   *2 marks*

                                                   Total 20 marks

6 Methods of training

1 B   **2** A   **3** D   **4** C   *4 marks*

5 **(a)** **i** Alternating periods of very hard exercise and rest. *Example*: repeated fast sprinting with rests   *2 marks*

         ii Using explosive movements. *Example*: bounding and hopping.   *2 marks*

     (b) **i** To be fast off the mark or fast gaining height to catch ball   *1 mark*

         ii Fast action with medium or light weights.   *1 mark*

     (c) **i** Frequency and Intensity   *2 marks*

         ii Type of training depends on particular fitness and skill requirements of each sport.   *2 marks*

                                                   Total 14 marks

Edexcel Sport Examined Teacher Support Pack © Beashel, Sibson and Taylor, Nelson Thornes Ltd, 2004

6 (a) To supply the working muscles with oxygen   *2 marks*

   (b) Constant pace running, swimming or similar activity   *2 marks*

   (c) Aerobic   *1 mark*

   (d) Sufficient oxygen is supplied to meet the needs of his training activity   *1 mark*

   (e) It gradually slows down   *1 mark*

   (f) Recovery period   *1 mark*

7 (a) Any two from: skill requirements of the sport, type of fitness needed, Carlos'
        training background, Carlos' present fitness level, type of training available   *2 marks*

   (b) Anaerobic   *1 mark*

   (c) 220–16=204

        60%–80% of 204 =120–160 beats per minute   *3 marks*

   (d) Interval training. *Example*: repeated alternating sprints and rests   *2 marks*

   (e)

Possible effects of training activity	Long runs	Weight training with heavy weights and few repetitions
Heart	*Any one from*: larger chambers, thicker wall, greater stroke volume, more complete chamber-emptying, lower resting heart rate, quicker recovery	Little or no effect
Muscular system	*Any one from*: more efficient aerobic systems, improved muscular endurance, slow twitch fibres increase in size, tendons stronger, ligaments more flexible	*Any one from*: increased muscular strength, muscle hypertrophy, fast twitch fibres increase in size, greater stores of glycogen, ATP and creatine phosphate in muscles, ligaments and tendons stronger

4 marks

Total 20 marks

7 Diet, health and hygiene

1 C   2 D   3 B   4 B   *4 marks*

5 (a) i   fats
       ii carbohydrates   *2 marks*

   (b)

Food type	Source of food type	Why it is important
	Any one from fruit, sugar, cereals etc.	Supply energy
Fat		Any two from: supply energy, keep us warm, keep skin in good condition
Protein	Any one from fish, meat, nuts	
Vitamins		Any one from: regulates body activities, helps working of muscles, helps release of energy from food

8 marks

Total 14 marks

6 (a) Carbohydrates and fats   *2 marks*

   (b) Any two from repair, growth, and efficient working of tissues   *2 marks*

   (c) Fibre is the indigestible part of the plant.   *1 mark*

        Any two from: adds bulk to food, aids digestion, prevents constipation,
        slows release of sugars.   *2 marks*

   (d) Anabolic steroids   *1 mark*

   (e) Any two from: aggression, acne, impotence, kidney disease   *2 marks*

   (f) diuretic   *1 mark*

7 (a) Any three from such as: desire to win/overcome injury/others are taking
        them/pressure to win/financial reasons   *3 marks*

   (b) Blood doping: returning blood to the body to increase number of red
        blood cells   *3 marks*

   (c) Increases number of red blood cells. Improves cardiovascular endurance,
        so allowing athlete to go faster for further.   *3 marks*

                                                                        Total 20 marks

8 Prevention and treatment of sports injuries

1 C   2 B   3 D   4 A   *4 marks*

5 (a) Appropriate rules relating to safety e.g. in cricket, batsman must wear helmets;
        protects batsman from head injury. No more than two bouncers in an over; reduces
        risk of batsman being hit.   *2 marks*

   (b) Accept answers similar to:

        – *Football*: leg injury – wear shin pads

        – *Javelin*: hit by javelin – rope off throwing area

        – *Canoeing*: drowning – wear lifejacket

        – *Cycling*: head injury when falling off – wear crash helmet

        – *Gymnastics*: awkward landing – always work on mats   *8 marks*

                                                                        Total 14 marks

6 (a) Any two from: gum shield, shin pads, gloves   *2 marks*

   (b) Any two from: hit by stick or ball, running into goal post, collision
        with player, uneven pitch   *2 marks*

   (c) Rest, Ice, Compression, Elevation   *4 marks*

   (d) Concussion   *1 mark*

   (e) *Danger* to casualty/First Aider; *Response*: is casualty conscious?
        Airway: is the airway open? *Breathing*: is the casualty breathing?
        Circulation: Is there a pulse?   *10 marks*

   (f) Recovery position   *1 mark*

                                                                        Total 20 marks

135

9 The circulatory system

1 B   **2** D   **3** A   **4** B   *4 marks*

5 **(a)** **i** Any three from: carries oxygen, removes carbon dioxide and waste, carries hormones, controls temperature and prevents infection   *3 marks*

       ii Collects oxygen and removes carbon dioxide   *2 marks*

   (b) Sends deoxygenated blood to the lungs   *1 mark*

   (c) Sends oxygenated blood around the body   *1 mark*

   (d) Receives deoxygenated blood from the body   *1 mark*

   (e) Any two from: age, exercise, stress, smoking diet and weight.   *2 marks*

Total 14 marks

6 **(a)** Prepares body for action or increases heart rate   *1 mark*

   (b) To transport more oxygen to the working muscles   *2 marks*

   (c) To take excess heat away from the body   *1 mark*

   (d) The volume of blood pumped out of the heart by each ventricle during one contraction   *1 mark*

       Stroke volume increases to meet the demands for oxygen from the working muscles.   *2 marks*

   (e) The heart beats more quickly or more deeply   *2 marks*

   (f) Insufficient blood supply to digest meal and supply oxygen to the working muscles during the race. Result is inferior performance   *2 marks*

   (g) Plasma, red blood cells, white blood cells, platelets   *4 marks*

   (h) Red blood cells: contain hæmoglobin which transports oxygen to working muscles   *3 marks*

   (i) The trained runner has stronger heart with greater stroke volume through training.   *2 marks*

Total 20 marks

10 The respiratory system

1 C   **2** A   **3** D   **4** C   *4 marks*

5 **(a)** *Intercostal muscles*: relax, allowing ribs to move downwards   *1 mark*

       diaphragm: relaxes, pushed back into domed position   *1 mark*

   (b) **i** 4%   *1 mark*

       ii Working muscles use oxygen and produce carbon dioxide as waste product to be expelled by lungs.   *2 marks*

   (c) Oxygen is used up by the working muscles to provide energy and therefore less in expired air.   *2 marks*

       i *Tidal volume*: the amount of air that can be breathed in and out of the lungs with one breath   *1 mark*

       ii During strenuous exercise more oxygen needed by working muscles, therefore tidal volume increases to meet the need for more air to go to lungs.   *2 marks*

Total 14 marks

5 (a) i Takes air to lungs   *1 mark*

     ii Thin walls allow for gaseous exchange   *1 mark*

     iii Reduce friction when lungs expand and contract.   *1 mark*

  (b) i Increases   *1 mark*

     ii Steady   *1 mark*

     iii Increases   *1 mark*

  (c) i Muscles need to get oxygen from air to start working   *2 marks*

     ii Working muscles need steady supply of oxygen to maintain work rate   *2 marks*

     iii Working muscle need additional supplies of oxygen to work harder for sprint   *2 marks*

  (d) i aerobic   *1 mark*

     ii anaerobic   *1 mark*

  (e) i insufficient oxygen available during strenuous exercise   *1 mark*

     ii causes tiredness in muscles   *1 mark*

     iii improves VO_2 Max and ability to tolerate higher levels of lactic acid.   *2 marks*

  (f) Any two from: increased rate of breathing and depth of breathing, greater vital capacity, more oxygen available in the lungs, improved VO_2 Max.   *2 marks*

Total 20 marks

11 Our skeletal system

1 C   **2** B   **3** D   **4** A   *4 marks*

5 (a) i For bone growth   *1 mark*

     ii Any one from such as milk, cheese, yoghurt   *1 mark*

  (b) i Fine movements   *1 mark*

     ii Protection or major muscle attachment   *1 mark*

     iii Protection or body shape.   *1 mark*

  (c) Any two from: constant running on hard surfaces, lifting heavy weights, strenuous contact sports   *2 marks*

  (d) Short limbs are an advantage for a gymnast.   *1 mark*

     Short limbs produce speed and power quickly, as needed in, for example, somersaults.   *2 marks*

Total 14 marks

6 (a) Any three from:

    – *Protection*: rib cage protects heart and lungs when tackled

    – *Support*: holds organs in place during violent movement

    – *Shape*: framework for different positions needed

    – *Movement*: attachment for muscles for action

    – *Produces blood*: essential for stamina required.   *6 marks*

  (b) Weight pushing against his shoulders is passed to his legs through a straight vertebral column to avoid injury.   *2 marks*

137

(c) *Order*: cervical, thoracic, lumbar, sacral, coccyx.   *2 marks*

(d) Back muscles are attached to them; they allow bending forward,
backward and side-to-side.   *2 marks*

(e) No effect on length of bones and therefore height.   *1 mark*

Regular training increases bone density and therefore bone strength.   *2 marks*

(f) Cartilage is changed to bone during growth, bone increases in length at the
growth plates, calcium is essential for growth and gives bones
their hardness.   *3 marks*

(g) Bone is in a constant state of regeneration and needs weight-bearing
exercise to maintain bone health.   *2 marks*

Total 20 marks

12 Joints, tendons and ligaments

1 B   2 D   3 A   4 C   *4 marks*

5 (a) i   Hinge

   ii Ball and socket   *2 marks*

   (b) i   Extension

   ii Flexion   *2 marks*

   (c) Cartilage   *1 mark*

   (d) i   Produces synovial fluid   *1 mark*

   ii Lubricates joint   *1 mark*

   iii Reduces friction   *1 mark*

   iv Holds bones together or protects joint   *1 mark*

   v   Hold bones together   *1 mark*

Total 14 marks

6 (a) Flexible joints essential for karate and improved range of movement   *2 marks*

   (b) i   Abduction   *1 mark*

   ii Adduction   *1 mark*

   iii Extension   *1 mark*

   iv Flexion   *1 mark*

   (c) i   Ball and socket   *1 mark*

   ii Hinge   *1 mark*

   (d) Deeper socket and stronger ligaments   *2 marks*

   (e) Attach muscle to bone and transmit muscular force   *2 marks*

   (f) i   Femur and tibia   *2 marks*

   ii Abduction and adduction   *2 marks*

   iii To keep bones of joint together   *1 mark*

   iv Improve strength of muscles surrounding joint   *1 mark*

   v   Any two from: healthy diet, strengthening muscles, regular exercise,
       flexibility exercises, warm-up and cool-down, training for sport.   *2 marks*

Total 20 marks

13 Muscles and muscle action

| 1 | B | 2 | A | 3 | D | 4 | A | | *4 marks* |

5   Trapezius – *example*: holding the head up in a rugby scrum   *2 marks*

    Flexes forearm – *example*: drawing bow in archery   *2 marks*

    Deltoids – Move arm in all directions   *2 marks*

    Gluteals – *example*: stepping up when climbing   *2 marks*

    Flex knee joint/point toes: *example*: running   *2 marks*

                                          Total 14 marks

6   **(a)** Any three from gastrocnemius, quadriceps, hamstrings, gluteals   *3 marks*

    (b) Any three from:

        – Gastrocnemius – *example*: heel raises   *1 mark*

        – Quadriceps – *example*: squats   *1 mark*

        – Hamstrings – *example*: leg curls   *1 mark*

        – Gluteals – *example*: squats   *1 mark*

    (c) Quadriceps and hamstrings   *2 marks*

    (d) **i** Fast twitch   *1 mark*

        ii Provide fast, powerful movements need for kicking, jumping, sprinting   *2 marks*

    (e) **i** *Kicking*: isotonic

        ii *Standing*: isometric   *2 marks*

    (f) To be ready to react quickly and to respond to position of ball and other players   *2 marks*

    (g) Hypertropy is muscle growth due to exercise.   *1 mark*

        Atrophy is loss of muscle mass due to inactivity.   *1 mark*

                                          Total 17 marks

Edexcel Sport Examined Teacher Support Pack © Beashel, Sibson and Taylor, Nelson Thornes Ltd, 2004